From Bitcoin to Burning Man and Beyond: The Quest for Identity and Autonomy in a Digital Society

From Bitcoin to Burning Man and Beyond
*The Quest for Identity and Autonomy
in a Digital Society*

*Edited by
John H. Clippinger
and
David Bollier*

*Published by ID3
in cooperation with Off the Common Books
2014*

ISBN 978-1-937146-58-0

Published by ID3
in cooperation with Off the Common Books, Amherst, Massachusetts.

Chapter 1, "Social Computing and Big Data, " by *Alex "Sandy" Pentland*, is
re-published here with the kind permission of Penguin Press, excerpted from
Pentland's book, *Social Physics: How Good Ideas Spread –
The Lessons from a New Science* (2014).

The Institute for Institutional Innovation by Data-Driven Design—ID3 – is an independent research and educational nonprofit 501(c)(3) based in Boston and affiliated with the M.I.T. Media Lab. Founded in 2011 by Dr. John Henry Clippinger and M.I.T. Professor Alex "Sandy" Pentland, ID3's mission is to develop an open data ecosystem through research, education and the support of an open source service platform, Open Mustard Seed (OMS). This endeavor seeks to address the severe infrastructural and governance limitations of existing institutions by giving individuals and groups greater control over their data, and the ability to deploy a new generation of trusted, decentralized, autonomous organizations and institutions globally.

Open Mustard Seed (OMS) is an open source platform that gives us genuine control over our own data. It lets us collect and share our personal information in a secure, transparent and accountable way, enabling authentic, trusted social and economic relationships to flourish. The system is dynamic and contextual, which means that we can share specific data at the appropriate time and place and with the people we want, and *only* them. By simply being ourselves, our data records generate unique, highly secure digital credentials—eliminating the need for passwords and repetitive log-ins. By helping us build decentralized autonomous organizations and trusted relationships, OMS enables groups to form and govern their own micro-economies—self-regulating, self-healing networks that can create their own forms of cooperation, including digital currencies, user-driven markets and social affinity groups. OMS is thus a new vehicle for us to build and scale our own interoperable communities of interest and markets – intimately, securely and at a global scale.

Contents

Part III: Open Architectures for an Open Society

Acknowledgments

SIMPLY STATED, THERE WOULD NOT HAVE been a ID3, Open Mustard Seed, or even this volume without the generous, three year support of RR Donnelley & Sons Company. Special gratitude is due to Tom Quinlan, the CEO of RR Donnelley & Sons Company, who has shown exceptional vision and leadership in his early support of ID3's open source mission long before personal data, Big Data, surveillance, and digital currencies were topics of keen public interest.

Special thanks is also due to the M.I.T. Media Lab as a research collaborator, and to Professor Alex (Sandy) Pentland, the cofounder of ID3, who has inaugurated a whole new area of research about personal data ecology and the social physics of human interaction. The ambition and rigor of Sandy's investigations into the social life of data has an ongoing impact on ID3's work and on the design of Open Mustard Seed

Finally, we would like to thank all those who contributed to this volume, and who were part of the Windhover Transition dialogues. The enthusiasm, goodwill and creativity that our colleagues freely volunteered in addressing the themes of this volume were truly impressive. We came away not only inspired, but deeply convinced that the future of identity, autonomy and trusted community will be pivotal issues in the years ahead.

Introduction

A CONSTANT THEME THROUGHOUT HUMAN HISTORY is a deep-seated yearning for a just, perfectible, and virtuous society. The recurrent challenge to this dream is *how* to achieve such a goal in a secular, imperfect world. For every optimistic vision (Plato's *Republic*, Jean-Jacques Rousseau's *Social Contract*, Ralph Waldo Emerson's very American ideal of "self reliance," Karl Marx classless society in *Communist Manifesto*, and B.F. Skinner's *Walden II*) and there is the countervailing pragmatist, even cynic's skepticism (Niccolo Machiavelli's *The Prince*, Samuel Butler's *Erewhon*). Inevitably, such grand visions become dashed against the hard realities of the inherent weaknesses, indeed archaic drives, of human nature.

These same tragic struggles are being played out today in Western societies, whose Enlightenment ideals of democratic rule seem to have run their course., A continuous flow of scientific findings are undermining many foundational claims about human rationality and perfectibility while exponential technological changes and exploding global demographics overwhelm the capacity of democratic institutions to rule effectively, and ultimately, their very legitimacy. Once-unimpeachable electoral processes have been corrupted, and hallowed institutional checks and balances circumvented. The age-old question of "Who guards the guards?" continues to confound humanity today as it did thousands of years ago.

This fundamental question of how to *design* effective self-governance is what many, if not most, of the authors of this volume attempt to answer, each in in his or her own way. How we might design more effective, transparent, accountable and self-healing institutions? As more of our personal and public lives become infused and shaped by data from sensors and computing devices, the distinctions between "the digital" and "the physical" have become increasingly blurred. From commerce and governance to education and social life, we are rapidly moving into an immersive societal ecology of data.

This transition raises not just new possibilities for rethinking and redesigning primary institutions, but, in truth, a new imperative. The seemingly intractable problems that our democratic nations have in achieving social equity and scalable and effective government are problems that stem, fundamentally, from deficient governance structures. Institutions that were invented in the 18th century are poorly equipped to deal with a 21st century society of instantaneous global communication, data-driven commerce, self-organized virtual communities and non-state digital currencies. The virtualization of so many basic functions of society, the rise of Big Data, and the ubiquity of computing essentially demand that we devise new rules or, better yet, new types of self-enforcing social contracts for all types of human interaction and governance.

Nowhere is this transition more pronounced than in the explosion of new ways to create and exchange money and to verify the identity of and monetize "digital assets." What once required the authority of a central bank or a sovereign authority can now be achieved through open, distributed crypto-algorithms. National borders, traditional legal regimes and human intervention are increasingly moot. Bitcoin's challenge to the banking world and Burning Man's challenge to social convention are not isolated phenomena. They are harbingers of an inexorable change in how all aspects human affairs are going to be conducted and governed. They point to new types of governance institutions, new, more participatory roles for individuals and communities, and a new ethic and worldview.

The rise of Bitcoin as the vanguard digital currency that can verify and securely clear transactions instantaneously and costlessly, is but the first salvo in an ongoing assault against legacy institutions – and not just financial institutions, but established institutions across all sectors. The efficiencies, convenience, accountability and pro-social potentials are simply too significant. Whether Bitcoin itself is here to stay, or is but the first round in an ongoing, colossal social and economic experimentation, remains to be seen.

What is clear is that we are seeing a new kind of highly distributed, self-governing infrastructure that profoundly alters one of the most fundamental precepts of human social and economic organization – the formal recognition and management of identities, access rights to resources and the management of risk. In this new data ecology, virtually anything can become a "digital asset" – identities, currencies, securities, contracts, mortgages, derivatives, goods, services, rewards, genome, licenses, titles, certificates, and much more. The identity, value and security of such assets can be verified through a variety of sophisticated new authentication and cryptographic methods such as OpenID Connect, OAuth 2, "zero knowledge proofs," Byzantine Fault Tolerance, Merkel Trees, and homographic encryption – opening the door for entirely new forms of social and market exchange.

This "datafication of everything" is already having significant ramifications for existing institutions of government, commerce and international relations. After all, when all significant digital transactions and behaviors can be logged and monitored – and existing institutions are proving ill-equipped to provide reliable, transparent governance and accountability – it is only natural that people will wish to develop new forms of digitally based regulation and governance. Rather than resorting to cumbersome and ineffectual forms of regulatory oversight and intervention, such as "notification and consent," "do not collect" lists and "data retention" directives, new digital platforms enable "performance based" regulation and governance that can use government- sanctioned algorithms and APIs to provide more effective, less corruptible, real-time oversight.

There are significant differences between this new "digital asset ecology" of the Internet and its "content and social media" predecessor. In social media, violations of privacy are often dismissed either as inexorable costs of modern life or nonconsequential matters – "get over it" events. But now the Internet has become a mission-critical infrastructure for all forms of health, defense, financial, transportation and sovereign interactions. As a result, privacy and security take on a whole new meaning, gravity and urgency when verifying and transporting trillions of dollars for Central Banks or in controlling military assets such as people, satellites and drones. Failures of privacy – that is, unwanted and illegitimate surveillance, and the subversion of trusted connections, controls, relationships and institutions – are not casual matters, "get over it" events. They directly affect national security, sovereignty, and the trust and wealth of pillar institutions, thereby potentially invoking the exercise of naked "kinetic" power.

The fusion of the physical and the digital in the new data ecology creates unprecedented opportunities for the design and testing of new kinds of *Decentralized Autonomous Organizations, Authorities and Enterprises*. Rather than have essential institutional functions (such as credentialing, enrollment, authentication, authorization, regulatory oversight, auditing, enforcement, dispute resolution, market making and clearing) be physical and human-dependent processes, it is now possible, indeed, even necessary, to make such processes digital, algorithmic, autonomous, transparent and self-correcting. This change not only raises the prospect for resolving the "who guards the guards" problem, it also has the potential to resolve a wide range of institutional challenges involving collective action, reputational integrity, systemic risk oversight, and the protected sharing of confidential data.

When traditional governance institutions and mechanisms are embedded in a data ecology, many forms of corruption, collusion, fraud, free riders, deception and coercion issues can be addressed through the "mechanism design" of institutions, policies and practices. These autonomous mechanisms can provably resolve, or at least, reduce the incidence of these failures. What until the present has had to be framed as an intractable "political matter" around oversight, fair representation, rule making and adjudication, can now be replaced or at least supplemented by algorithms and software agents with highly focused, independent and accountable human oversight.

From this perspective, institutional and regulatory design challenges become "performance and evidence based" – not ideological or subject to hidden special interests. In this sense, the design of institutional and governance mechanisms become a new category of social technology, one that is replicable, testable, scalable, and potentially a beneficiary of the "magic" of Moore's Law. It is hard to imagine a future in which governance is not regarded as an inevitable cost and source of failure, but rather a variable cost subject to technological innovation, and itself a creator of value!

The Institute for Institutional Innovation by Data-Driven Design, or ID3, was formed in 2011 as an independent research and educational nonprofit 501(c)(3) based in Boston affiliated with the M.I.T. Media Lab. ID3's mission is to develop an open data ecosystem through research, education and the support of an open source service platform, Open Mustard Seed (OMS). This endeavor seeks to address the severe infrastructural and governance limitations of existing institutions by giving individuals and groups greater control over their data, and the ability to deploy a new generation of trusted, decentralized, autonomous organizations and institutions globally.

The Plan of This Book

This volume represents the contributions of eighteen different authors, many of whom have been involved with ID3 since its inception three years ago. The majority of the contributors attended a retreat last year in Jefferson, New Hampshire, where many of the topics discussed in this volume were discussed and debated. Out of that retreat emerged a shared sense of purpose and vision among the attendees that is reflected in a digital manifesto called *The Windhover Transition*, (see the Conclusion), named after John Clippinger's nearby farm.

From Bitcoin to Burning Man and Beyond is organized into three parts, representing three essential perspectives on how a new digital ecology might evolve. Part I, "Charting the New Ecology of Data," provides an introductory framework for understanding the power of distributed computing, the growth of mass participation and the rise of Big Data as a standard element – all of which are converging to create new sorts of institutions, governance and even human identity.

One of the most important innovations to arise from these trends is explored in Part II, "Digital Currencies as Instruments for Social Change." This part of the book describes the importance of complementary currencies, the significance of Bitcoin, and the other potentially transformative currencies that are now emerging, including the Ven, the proposed Impala for Africa and Green Coins to foster environmental improvements.

Finally, Part III, "Open Architectures for an Open Society," explores some of the conceptual and technical design issues that must be addressed in building an open, stable, civically robust and innovation-friendly future. The essays of this section build on the logic of the first two sections by explaining the importance of holistic system design ("holonics"), the lessons of self-governance for common-pool resources, and the ways in which Open Mustard Seed – the new software platform developed by ID3 – seeks to empower users to control their own data and build their own trusted governance systems.

The New Ecology of Data

While traditional Enlightenment notions regard the rational individual as the basic unit of a democratic polity and the economy, Professor Alex "Sandy" Pentland of the Human Dynamics Group at the M.I.T. Media Lab has found in his empirical research that social action and choice have other sources, effectively challenging and discrediting many core Enlightenment assumptions.

Using data analytic and machine learning methods to analyze voice, text, and face-to-face interactions on mobile social networks, Pentland shows in Chapter 1 that human learning and collective action are more often than not influenced by one's peers and colleagues than by "rationality" or "individual choice." Pentland is currently pioneering a new discipline, "Social Physics," whose goal is to identify the rules and "laws" the govern collective behavior and learning.

These issues are especially timely because the world has seen a remarkable proliferation of peer-to-peer software, services and other activities. As I outline in Chapter 2, "Why Self-Sovereignty Matters," there is a new breed of services and protocols that I call *The ODESS Stack*, with ODESS standing for "Open–Distributed–Emergent–Secure–Self-Reflexive. ODESS modes of software and services are immensely popular because they do not require external institutional authorities – i.e., corruptible human third parties – to function effectively. Rather they are "self-reflexive" in that they contain within themselves the necessary mechanisms to host, verify and clear transactions, and to audit themselves and self-correct errors and breaches. Their very design prevents them from violating their own operational policies, and as a result, they are highly resistant to outside manipulation and intrusion.

This theme is explored further in David Bollier's and John Clippinger's essay, "The Next Big Internet Disruption: Authority and Governance," in Chapter 3. The crux of this piece is the insight by David Reed, formerly of the M.I.T. Media Lab, that on open networks such as the Internet, greater value is generated through groups that are progressively more coherent and collaborative – or what Reed calls "Group Forming Networks," or GFNs. While the lowest level of value-creation occurs through a *broadcasting* model based on "best content," and a higher level of value can be generated through a network of *peer-to-peer transactions* based on collectives with the "most members," the most valuable networks, says Reed, are those that *facilitate group affiliations*.

If we apply the logic of Reed's thinking to contemporary circumstances, it is clear that the best way to unlock enormous stores of value on networks is to develop tools that can facilitate GFNs. As Bollier and Clippinger write: "This will be the next great Internet disruption. But to achieve this, we must develop a network architecture and software systems that can build trust and social capital in user-centric, scalable ways." A good way to help the Internet achieve its true growth and value potential is to adopt new mechanisms for authentication and governance. As a starting point, Bollier and Clippinger point to the eight design principles for managing commons-pool resources that the late Nobel Laureate Elinor Ostrom identified after decades of studying such forms of governance.

This theme – the principles of self-governance, or "decentralized autonomous organization" (DAO) – recurs in other chapters in the book. It is seen most notably in Peter Hirshberg's history of the Burning Man festival, in Chapter 5, and Jeremy Pitt's and Ada Diaconescu's essay, "The Algorithmic Governance of Common-Pool Resources," in Chapter 12. Any successful commons, according to Ostrom's design principles, must be able to define the boundaries of its community and governance; align the governance rules with local needs and conditions; and ensure that those affected by the rules can participate in modifying the rules. People must also be able to monitor compliance with rules, sanction free riders and vandals, and provide low-cost systems for resolving disputes – among other principles.

As these opening chapters suggest, the new environment of open networks places a premium on *relational* patterns among people instead of simply *transactional* ones. In a more transparent, fluid environment, the character of a community's culture takes on much greater significance. In Chapter 4, Maurizio Rossi argues in "The New Mestieri Culture of Artisans" that "each individual is becoming a peer in a larger community – a personal producer and entrepreneur who uses a variety of platforms to carry on a variety of relationships – not just among humans, but with machines."

Rossi sees this as contributing to a revival of artisan culture, the *Mestieri*, which still thrives in his home country, Italy, through its emphasis on craftsmanship and high design. He sees artisan culture becoming "supremely efficient, not to mention customer-friendly, because its design, production and retailing will take advantage of the modularity made possible by open networks." Rossi also sees branding itself as changing, becoming less propriety and closed, and more open – something that is not owned exclusively by a company, but belonging to the "collaborative community of artisans, companies, suppliers and customers, all of whom participate in the shared ecosystem." He contends that "open brands will have a social authenticity – a credibility and depth – that is rarely associated with branded products today."

The importance of culture in the new modes of self-governance is underscored as well by Peter Hirshberg in his fascinating profile of the Burning Man festival in the Nevada desert. Now twenty-eight years old, the annual Burning Man gathering attracts more than 60,000 people from around the world for a week-long encampment, celebration and participation in a "pop-up city." Hirshberg chronicles the evolution of Burning Man from a somewhat chaotic, "Mad Max" kind of anarchy to a robust, thriving transformational community that is influencing all sorts of "real world" innovations in urban design and self-governance.

"Once we eliminated firearms, invented the Greeters, repurposed and reorganized the Rangers, created a street grid, regulated traffic, increased population densities, and gave everyone an address," said founder Larry Harvey, "people could more freely interact; theme camps tripled, villages thrived, entire neighborhoods began to come alive."

Though a decentralized and anarchistic community, Burning Man also learned the importance of intense centralized planning and shared culture as ways to enable the flourishing of decentralized participation. Burning Man's Ten Principles offer valuable guidance to those who wish to build the world anew, by declaring the importance of radical inclusion, a culture of unconditional gift-giving, an ethic of decommodification and non-commercialism, radical self-reliance, radical self-expression and civic responsibility, among other principles.

Digital Currencies as Instruments for Social Change

In Part II, we shift gears by focusing on the dramatic proliferation of digital currencies in contemporary life. This is exemplified most vividly by Bitcoin, but it can also be seen in many other digital currencies, from Ripple to Ven to the M-Pesa.

While the new currencies may be disruptive and in some instances troubling (such as the money-laundering capabilities of Bitcoin), they are also pioneering some new, more efficient and socially constructive mechanisms of exchange.

In Chapter 6, "The Internet of Money," Irving Wladawsky-Berger, a veteran of innovation and strategy at IBM who is now Strategic Advisor to Citi, provides an excellent introduction to the phenomenon of digital currencies and the regulatory and business issues they raise. The new currencies are remarkable in their capacity to "decentralize trust" with advanced cryptographic techniques and distribut-ed architectures; the money does not require third-party authorities to vouch for the security and integrity of the currencies themselves. But this also creates vexing policy issues because the new currencies are an unprecedented new kind of asset class – digital assets – that can be valued and exchanged on a global scale.

Regulators are challenged as to how to classify digital currencies. On the one hand the Internal Revenue Service has classified Bitcoin as a kind of property and asset, whose increases and decreases in val-ue have to be accounted for and taxes paid on. Given that Bitcoin has been rather volatile in its history, this classification makes it impracti-cal to use as a payment currency. The office of the U.S. Treasury De-partment, which regulates money, on the other had, classifies Bitcoin as a currency, which thereby requires that it comply with Know Your Customer (KYC) and Anti-Money Laundering (AML) regulations. It seems that Bitcoin occupies the worst of both worlds!

It will take time and ingenuity for existing systems of money to accommodate the newcomers, but as Bernard Lietaer reminds us, we should welcome a diversification of currencies in the world economy. In Chapter 7, Lietar makes the important observation that *efficiency* in complex flow systems like money must be balanced with *resilience*, defined as the capacity to adapt to changes in the environment and survive serious disruptions. This is the essence of sustainability.

Seen in this holistic perspective, a monoculture of currencies is dangerously unstable because "an excessive focus on efficiency will tend to create exactly the kind of bubble economy that we have been able to observe repeatedly in every boom and bust cycle in his-tory...." If we regard the global monetary system as a "complex flow system," Lietaer observes, then we can see that its sustainability is based on "the emergent properties of its structural diversity and in-terconnectivity." For the monetary system, this suggests the need for governments to move away from "a monoculture of a single type of money," and begin to accept other types of currencies, besides con-ventional bank-debt national money.

Three additional chapters explore the fascinating capabilities of specific currency innovations. Jonathan Ledgard, Director of Future Africa at the Swiss Federal Institute of Technology, and Africa correspondent-at-large for *The Economist*, proposes the creation of a pan-African digital currency that would use peer-to-peer technology to enable low-value transactions via smartphones. As Ledgard explains in Chapter 8, the currency could be adapted to local contexts but in any case would help users build credit histories to secure micro-loans for schooling, healthcare and housing. It could also be used by governments and aid agencies to verify their disbursements of money in more accurate, inexpensive ways.

In Chapter 9, Stan Stalnaker, the founding director of Hub Culture and Ven currency, describes the origins of Ven, the first real digital currency – founded in 2007 – and now an Internet reserve currency. As a commodity-backed currency, Ven are notable for their stable value, global reach, security and support for green initiatives. In Chapter 10, the idea of a green currency – Green Coins – is proposed by former FCC Chairman Reed E. Hundt who is now CEO of the Coalition for Green Capital, and his associates at the Coalition, Jeffrey Schub and Joseph R. Schottenfeld. Working through the nonprofit Coalition for Green Capital, the authors are exploring how a solar cryptocurrency based on some of the design principles of Bitcoin, especially a distributed ledger, might be used to incentivize the adoption of solar power, especially among homeowners.

Open Architectures for an Open Society

The final section of *From Bitcoin to Burning Man and Beyond* contemplates the design architectures on open networks that are needed to improve institutional performance and enhance individual freedom while bolstering the entire system's stability and resilience. These issues are examined in some of the preceding chapters, especially Bernard Lietaer's chapter on complex systems and currencies, but here the authors focus on system protocols and software design.

Holonics theorist Mihaela Ulieru opens Part III by introducing the logic of holonic systems in Chapter 11. She writes: "A recurrent problem is our failure to understand that human endeavors are part of holistic, living systems, natural and constructed, whose constitutive elements are mutually defining, expressive and constantly evolving. In actual circumstances, the individual cannot be cast as against, below or above the group; the individual is in fact nested *within* dynamic forms of social organization. Living organisms have subjectivities, inter-subjectivities and behaviors that are nested within larger living systems."

Once we accept this general scenario as real, it has profound implications for the (misleading) Newtonian conception of the universe and its cause-and-effect logic and crude narratives. Ulieru's mission as a holonics scholar is to jolt us out of our conventional understandings of physical and human dynamics, and point us to the complex, dynamic rules and laws of self-organizing systems. She helps us to understand the limitations of organizational hierarchies and to appreciate institutions as *living systems* embedded in larger social and ecological contexts.

By adopting this perspective, we can begin to blend multiple scientific and humanistic disciplines and focus on the role of the *holarchy* to understand how emergent, self-organized agents can collaborate in advancing a common purpose. Ulieru is giving us a richer theoretical understanding of what happens on the World Wide Web every day. The challenge is how we might use these principles to build more effective organizations, foster ecological stewardship and unleash more generative human relationships.

Jeremy Pitt and Ada Diaconescu, computer scientists at Imperial College London and Telecom ParisTech, respectively, offer a fascinating analysis of how they are applying Elinor Ostrom's design principles for the allocation of common-pool resources to the design of software. Their engineering goal is to provide "an algorithmic basis for governance of common-pool resources in electronic social systems." In Chapter 12, Pitt and Diaconescu explain their interest in blending the capabilities of software platforms with the dynamics of living social systems, resulting in "socio-technical systems" that embody the ODESS principles (Open–Distributed–Emergent–Secure–Self-Reflexive) described by John H. Clippinger earlier in the book.

This is not an easy challenge, but it is a direction that is validated by Professor Ostrom's study of common-pool resources, people's actual behaviors on open platforms, and the value proposition of networks described by theorist David Reed, as noted.

So how to devise an information-communications technology framework that can implement Ostrom's rules? Pitt and Diaconescu argue that we need to devise algorithmic frameworks as a "meso-level of governance" that can mediate between micro-levels of self-organized governance and macro-level outcomes that may be incoherent or undesirable. This could be the basis for a new kind of "social ergonomics" on self-governance platforms.

Open Mustard Seed, or OMS, is a bold attempt to fulfill many of the principles outlined by Ulieru, Pitt and Diaconescu, among other theorists. OMS aims to become a versatile platform for people to develop their own ODESS-based social ecosystems on open networks. The centerpiece of OMS is its capacity to let people share all their personal data within a legally constituted "trust framework" and self-initiated "personal data stores" (PDS) that can securely store and process data about themselves.

The general technical framework of OMS is outlined in Chapter 13 by Thomas Hardjono, Technical Lead and Executive Director of the M.I.T. Consortium for Kerberos and Internet Trust; Patrick Deegan, Chief Technology Officer of ID3 and Lead Architect of OMS; and John H. Clippinger, Executive Director and CEO of ID3 and Research Scientist at the M.I.T. Media Lab Human Dynamics Group. Hardjono et al. describe how the various elements of the trust framework – open authentication, storage, discovery, payment, auditing, market making and monetized "app store" services – all work together in an integrated fashion. What makes OMS so distinctive is its "privacy by design" principles – that is, absolute privacy, security and trusted exchange are built into the very design of the system.

In Chapter 14, Chief Technology Officer of ID3 Patrick Deegan takes us more deeply into the theoretical and operational principles behind OMS. In "The Relational Matrix," Deegan notes that the Internet's initial architecture made no provisions for a secure, viable identity infrastructure or the means by which individuals could assert control over their personal data. He argues that because the current infrastructure cannot be simply uprooted and replaced, any envisioned "authentication, privacy and sharing layer" has to grow organically on top of the existing layer. Fortunately, this is now possible by combining technologies for the self-deployment and administration of services with new encryption, identity authentication and access controls technologies and protocols. The Open Mustard Seed (OMS) platform represents an open source effort to enable such an architecture on a global scale.

To assure that these new types of self-organized governance can take root and blossom on the Web, Harry Halpin argues that the logic of digitization and open networks requires a "new grammar" of open standards to assure that freedom and innovation can flourish. Halpin is Research Scientist at the World Wide Web Consortium (W3C/M.I.T.), where he leads efforts in cryptography and social standards. Halpin writes that an open social Web is critical to the future of self-organized behaviors and secure digital identity: "To prevent the centralization of our data in the hands of a neo-feudal digital regime and all the dangers that this entails, we urgently need to construct a new ecosystem of open standards to allow secure forms of digital identity that everyone from individuals to institutions can deploy without being 'locked-in' to existing players."

The Windhover Transition

In August 2013, ID3 invited fifteen leading thinkers, programmers, tech experts and entrepreneurs to meet for a three-day retreat in Jefferson, New Hampshire, to try to name, capture and distill the logic of the digital culture now emerging. This book is one result of that convocation; another, far more succinct result was The Windhover Transition. This statement was an attempt to describe the broad, general contours of the transition that we are now experiencing and issue a call to step up to meet its promise and challenges.

This book concludes, therefore, with that manifesto. It is our hope that the Windhover Transition statement and this book will help reframe some of the conversations about the future and stimulate new initiatives to actualize the vision that so many of us see. The details of the emerging paradigm and many of its elements are not entirely clear. Yet the deeper principles and prevailing trends seem quite powerful and demonstrable, and lead us to the major question: How soon will we recognize these deeper currents and reorient our energies and imaginations to take advantage of them?

John H. Clippinger
David Bollier
ID3
Boston, Massachusetts
June 1, 2014

Part I

CHARTING THE NEW ECOLOGY OF DATA

Chapter 1

Social Physics and the Human Centric Society

By Alex Pentland

THE FREE MARKET MODEL FOR SOCIETY has its roots in 18th-century notions of natural law: the idea that humans are self-interested and self-commanded and that they relentlessly seek to gain from the exchange of goods, assistance and favors in all social transactions. Open competition for such theoretical individuals is a natural way of life, and if all the costs (e.g., pollution, waste) are taken into account, then the dynamics of open competition can result in an efficient society. As Adam Smith explained:

> They are led by an invisible hand to make nearly the same distribution of the necessaries of life, which would have been made, had the earth been divided into equal portions among all its inhabitants, and thus without intending it, without knowing it, advance the interest of the society, and afford means to the multiplication of the species.[1]

The power of markets to distribute resources efficiently—together with the assumption that humans are relentless competitors—is the bedrock of most modern societies. It works well for stocks and commodities, and reasonably well for wages and housing. The contemporary trend is to apply market thinking to *all* sectors of society. But does this 18th-century understanding of human nature truly form a good model for all of these sectors of our modern society? I think not.

The Real World Isn't A Market, It Is An Exchange Network

Perhaps the major flaw in the free-market view of human nature is that people are not simply self-interested, self-commanded individuals. What we are interested in, and our command mechanism itself, is overwhelmingly determined by social norms created by interactions with other people. Modern science now understands that cooperation is just as important and just as prevalent in human society as competition. Our friends watch our backs in sports and business teammates cooperate to win against other teams, and everywhere people support family, children and the elderly. In fact, the main source of competition in society may not be among individuals but rather among cooperating groups of peers

Moreover, recent economics research has shown that the basic assumption within classic market thinking—that there are many sellers and buyers that can be substituted for each other easily—does not apply even to economies such as that of the U.S.[2] Instead, we should think of the economy as an *exchange network*: a complex web of specific exchange relationships. In fact the idea of a market, in which it is imagined that all the participants can see and compete evenly with everyone else, is almost always an oversimplification. In reality some people have better connections, some people know more than others, and some purchases are more difficult than others, due to distance, timing, or other secondary considerations.

Just as financial markets and the invisible hand are an oversimplification, so is the idea that political competition produces a "market of ideas" that somehow results in good government. Political or economic labels such as "bourgeoisie," "working class," "libertarian" are often inaccurate stereotypes of groups of people who actually have widely varying individual characteristics and desires. As a result, reasoning about society in terms of classes or parties is imprecise and can lead to mistaken overgeneralizations. In the real world, a group of people develops deeply similar norms only when they have both strong interactions and they recognize each other as peers.

Modern Natural Law: Exchanges, Not Markets

Why is the real world made up of exchange networks rather than markets? In a word: *trust*.

Relationships in an exchange network quickly become stable (we go back again and again to the person who gives us the best deal), and with stability comes trust, i.e., the expectation of a continued valuable relationship. This is different than in a typical market, where a buyer may deal with a different seller every day as prices fluctuate. In exchange networks, buyers and sellers can more easily build up the trust that makes society resilient in times of great stress. In markets, one must usually rely on having access to an accurate reputation mechanism that rates all the participants, or to an outside referee to enforce the rules.

This insight comes from what I call *social physics*: using game theory to mathematically examine the properties of human societies, such as comparing a society based on exchange networks with one based on markets. For instance, the equations from the thesis of my PhD student Ankur Mani show that the dynamics of exchange networks structurally favor fair outcomes, with the surplus generated by the relationship equally divided between the individuals involved. [3] As a consequence of fairness, there is more stability and greater levels of trust. Exchange networks are also more cooperative, robust and resilient to outside shocks. Social physics provides a good recipe for building a society that will survive.

Adam Smith thought that the invisible hand was due to a market mechanism that was constrained by peer pressure within the community. In the succeeding centuries we have tended to emphasize the market mechanism and forgotten the importance of the peer pressure part of his idea. Social physics strongly suggests that the invisible hand is more due to the trust, cooperation and robustness properties of the person-to-person network of exchanges than it is due to any magic in the workings of the market. If we want to have a fair, stable society, we need to look to the network of exchanges between people, and not to market competition.

How can we move from a market-centric to a human-centric society?

So how does this idea of an exchange society apply to modern life? Today we have mass media to spread information, and our much higher levels of mobility allow us to interact with many more people. Information is so universally available and our social networks are extremely broad. Do these facts mean that we have transitioned from an exchange society to a market society? I think the answer is no.

Even though we now have much greater breadth and rate of interaction, our habits still depend mostly on interactions with a few trusted sources—those people whom we interact with frequently—and for each person the number of such trusted individuals remains quite small. In fact, the evidence is that the number of trusted peers that we have today is pretty much the same as it was tens of thousands of years ago.[4]

This small, relatively stable network of trusted peers still dominates our habits of eating, spending, entertainment, political behavior—and technology adoption. Similarly, face-to-face social ties drive output in companies and accounts for the productivity and creative output of the largest cities. This means that the spread of new behaviors throughout society is still dominated by local, person-to-person exchanges even in the presence of modern digital media and modern transportation. We still live in an exchange society, albeit one with much greater levels of exploration.

How can we use these insights about human nature to design a society better suited to human nature? Economic theory still provides a useful template for shaping our society, but we have to begin with a more accurate notion of human nature. Because we are not just economic creatures, our vision of a human-centric society must include a broader range of human motivations—such as curiosity, trust, and social pressure.

Social physics suggests that the first step is to focus on *the flow of ideas* rather than on the flow of wealth, since the flow of ideas is the source of both cultural norms and innovation. A focus on improving idea flow, rather than financial flows, will allow individuals to make better decisions and our society to develop more useful behavioral norms. A key insight from social physics is that it is critical that the flow and exchange of ideas be inclusive, because insufficiently diverse idea flow leads to rigid and insular societies, and insular communities (including the society of Adam Smith's time) often inflict terrible damage on weaker communities with whom they share resources.

Idea Flow

Idea flow is the spreading of ideas, whether by example or story, through a social network—be it a company, a family, or a city. Being part of this flow of ideas allows people to learn new behaviors without the dangers or risks of individual experimentation. People can also acquire large integrated patterns of behavior without having to form them gradually through laborious experimentation.

In fact, humans rely so much on our ability to learn from the ideas that surround us that some psychologists refer to us as *Homo imitans*. The collective intelligence of a community comes from idea flow; we learn from the ideas that surround us, and others learn from us. Over time, a community with members who actively engage with each other creates a group with shared, integrated habits and beliefs. Idea flow depends upon social learning, and indeed, this is the basis of social physics: Our behavior can be predicted from our exposure to the example behaviors of other people.

Because "idea flow" takes into account the variables of a social network structure, the strength of social influence between people, and individual susceptibilities to new ideas, it also serves another vital role: It gives a reliable, mathematical prediction of how changing any of these variables will change the performance of all the people in the network. Thus, the mathematical framework of idea flow allows us to tune social networks in order to make better decisions and achieve better results.

For example, what can be done when the flow of ideas becomes either too sparse and slow or too dense and fast? How does the "exploration" process—using social networks to search for ideas and then winnow them down to just a few good ones—result in a harvest of ideas that produces good decisions? Is this just a random recombination of ideas with little contribution from our individual intelligences, or are there strategies that are critical to successful exploration? The mathematics of social physics lets us answer these questions.

How Can We Harvest the Best Ideas?

The exploration process is fundamentally a search for new ideas within one's social network, so to understand how to find the best ideas I launched two big data studies that contain almost two million hours of interaction data covering everyone within two communities for a total of over two years. These studies allowed me to build quantitative, predictive models of how we humans find and incorporate new ideas into our decisions.

The studies paint a picture of humans as sailors. We all sail in a stream of ideas, ideas that are the examples and stories of the peers who surround us; exposure to this stream shapes our habits and beliefs. We can resist the flow if we try, and even choose to row to another stream, but most of our behavior is shaped by the ideas we are exposed to. The idea flow within these streams binds us together into a sort of collective intelligence, one comprised of the shared learning of our peers.

The continual exploratory behavior of humans is a quick learning process that is guided by apparent popularity among peers. In contrast, adoption of habits and preferences is a slow process that requires repeated exposure and perceptual validation within a community of peers. Our social world consists of the rush and excitement of new ideas harvested through exploration, and then the quieter and slower process of engaging with peers in order to winnow through those ideas, to determine which should be converted into personal habits and social norms.

I think of organizations as a group of people sailing in a stream of ideas. Sometimes they are sailing in swift, clear streams where the ideas are abundant, but sometimes they are in stagnant pools or terrifying whirlpools. At other times, one person's idea stream forks off, splitting it apart from other people and taking them in a new direction. To me, this is the real story of community and culture; the rest is just surface appearance and illusion.

When the flow of ideas incorporates a constant stream of outside ideas as well, then the individuals in the community make better decisions than they could on their own. To bring new ideas into a work group or community, however, there are three main things to remember:

Social learning is critical. Copying other people's successes, when combined with individual learning, is dramatically better than individual learning alone. When your individual information is unclear, rely more on social learning; when your individual information is strong, rely less on social learning.

One disturbing implication of these findings is that our hyper-connected world may be moving toward a state in which there is too much idea flow. In a world of echo chambers, fads and panics are the norm, and it is much harder to make good decisions. We need to pay much more attention to where our ideas are coming from, and we should actively discount common opinions and keep track of the contrarian ideas. (We can build software tools to help us do this automatically, but to do so we have to keep track of the provenance of ideas.)

Contrarians are important. When people are behaving independently of their social learning, it is likely that they have independent information and that they believe in that information enough to fight the effects of social influence. Find as many of these "wise guys" as possible and learn from them.

Such contrarians sometimes have the best ideas, but sometimes they are just oddballs. How can you know which is which? If you can find many such independent thinkers and discover that there is a consensus among a large subset of them, then a really, really good strategy is to follow the "contrarian consensus."

Diversity is important. When everyone is going in the same direction, then it is a good bet that there isn't enough diversity in your information and idea sources, and you should explore further. A big danger of social learning is groupthink. To avoid groupthink and echo chambers, you have to compare what the social learning suggests with what isolated individuals (who have only external information sources) are doing. If the so-called common sense from social learning is just an overconfident version of what isolated people think, then you are likely in a groupthink or echo chamber situation. In this case, a surprisingly good strategy is to bet against the common sense.

But it is also important to diversify by considering more than one strategy at a time because, as our environment changes, the old strategies stop working and new strategies take the lead. Therefore, it is not the strategies that have been most successful that you want to follow; it is really the strategies that *will be* most successful that you have to find. And since predicting the future is hard, diversification of social learning is important.

In summary, people act like idea-processing machines combining individual thinking and social learning from the experiences of others. Success depends greatly on the quality of your exploration and that, in turn, relies on the diversity and independence of your information and idea sources. By harvesting from the parts of our social network that touch other streams, that is, by crossing what sociologist Ron Burt called the "structural holes" within the fabric of society, we can create innovation. When we choose to dip into a different stream, we bring up new habits and beliefs, and it is these innovations that help us make better decisions, and help our community to thrive.

Alex Pentland directs M.I.T.'s Human Dynamics Laboratory and the M.I.T. Media Lab Entrepreneurship Program, and co-leads the World Economic Forum Big Data and Personal Data Initiatives. His research group and entrepreneurship program have spun off more than thirty companies to date. In 2012 Forbes named Pentland one of the seven most powerful data scientists in the world.

This chapter is excerpted from Social Physics: How Good Ideas Spread – The Lessons from a New Science *(Penguin Press, 2014) with permission.*

Notes

[1] Smith, A., *Theory of Moral Sentiments* (First Edition, 1759; Penguin Classics, 2009).

[2] Acemoglu, D., V. Carvalho, A. Ozdaglar, and A. Tahbaz-Salehi, "The Network Origins of Aggregate Fluctuations," *Econometrica* 80 (5), pp. 1977–2016 (2012).

[3] Mani, A., A. Pentland, and A. Ozdalgar, "Existence of Stable Exclusive Bilateral Exchanges in Networks" (2010). See http://hd.media.mit.edu/tech-reports/TR-659.pdf.

[4] Dunbar, R., "Neocortex Size as a Constraint on Group Size in Primates," *Journal of Human Evolution* 20(6), pp. 469-493 (1992).

Chapter 2

Why Self-Sovereignty Matters

By John H. Clippinger

IT HAS BEEN SAID THAT "HE who enrolls, controls." Any "authoritative" party that defines and selectively confers "credentials" to access valued resources, privileges and rights – e.g., a bank, state, religious body or social website – exercises enormous power, often with little democratic oversight. Since such powers are extremely difficult to oversee and regulate, they eventually become a point of institutional failure. The old adage *Who guards the guards themselves? (Quis custodiet ipsos custodes?)* ultimately rears its ugly head and the "guards" become the overlords, a clique of self-perpetuating, self-serving beneficiaries. It is a historically tried dictum that the human oversight of human frailties inevitably succumbs to human frailties.

The Rise of Self-Correcting, Evolvable Institutions

In the struggle to give people greater dignity and control over their online lives (which increasingly encompass their offline lives as well), the classic institutions of authority – financial, educational, enterprise, religious, governmental – are failing. They are variously too slow, hierarchical, corrupted or socially disconnected to perform their assigned tasks as conscientious policymakers and respected guardians of their segment of the social order.

This failure of authoritative institutions constitutes one of the biggest challenges to human freedom in the digital era. It is such a fundamental point of failure across all sectors that it is unlikely to be resolved within existing institutional structures.[1] Yet growing public alarm over unchecked governmental and corporate surveillance and control is spurring the quest for innovative forms of governance that can effectively protect and express human rights.

A case in point is the "alpha geek" community's enthusiasm for Bitcoin, Ripple, digital currencies and encrypted peer-to-peer services. These services and protocols are instances of what I call *The ODESS Stack* (Open-Distributed-Emergent-Secure-Self-Reflexive), a set of distinctive software endowed with autonomous features. The fervent popularity of ODESS services arises from the fact that they do not require external institutional authorities – i.e., corruptible human third parties – to function. Rather they are "self-reflexive" in that they contain within themselves the necessary mechanisms to host, verify and clear transactions, and to audit themselves and self-correct errors and breaches. By virtue of their inherent design, they cannot violate their own policies and they are highly fortified against outside manipulation and intrusion. In Bitcoin's case, this means that it will issue no more than 21 million bitcoins and it will have a "block chain" register that is complete and transparent. To their supporters, these "algorithmic" "math-based institutions" are more trustworthy than their flesh-and-blood counterparts, such as Central Banks and governments.

It is tempting to dismiss the interest in ODESS protocols and services as a simple case of Digital Libertarianism, especially because there is certainly an Ayn Rand faction within these circles. But the ODESS approach to authority and legitimacy really transcends the traditional left/right ideological spectrum. The growing shift to algorithmically complete and self-contained services represents a more pragmatic, performance-based approach to governance and institutional design. In systems that are inherently experimental, empirical and technologically based, traditional ideological presumptions have little standing. Pragmatic outcomes and personal empowerment are the *sine qua non*.

ODESS protocols and platforms are really outgrowths of a new generation of communications and control technologies. It turns out that the convergence of open platforms, social networking, Big Data and encryption innovations allows us to address many social and economic problems that simply could not be seen or addressed under the regnant system of authoritative institutions.

Never before has it been possible to self-consciously design and test at scale new forms of social technologies with rapid iterations and innovation. Before it was possible to represent and express human activities digitally, the social and economic sciences were profoundly constrained in what they could imagine theoretically or test experimentally. This is no longer the case. Now it is possible to self-consciously design and test at scale new forms of social technologies with rapid iterations and ongoing improvements. Much of today's large-scale social and economic innovation is not being done within academia or government, but by technologically innovative companies that have the sophistication to exploit open networks, social networking and Big Data.

The automation of key control functions in trains, missiles, planes, boats and cars is already upon us, and fully autonomous terrestrial and aerial drones are not that far off. The march of autonomous control and self-organizing technologies is leading to a whole new class of services and protocols that obviate the need for traditional "authoritative" institutions for governance and control. Instead of presuming the need for active human oversight, whether through physical, regulatory or legal means, the goal that is emerging among so many ODESS systems is autonomic design: social and economic control/governance mechanisms that are intended to perform to an explicit standard and that can correct and improve their performance when they fail. Self-adaptive machine learning makes it possible for systems to learn from their mistakes and evolve to improve their performance.

In the face of institutional failures, respectable opinion generally focuses on reforming traditional "democratic" processes such as voting, legislation, adjudication, licensing, litigation and regulatory procedures. But these modes of governance are increasingly ineffective artifacts of a bygone era. They presume social realities that may not exist (perfect information, rational consumers) while failing to take account of ubiquitous new realities such as socially driven behavior using digital technologies on open networks.

Fortunately, ODESS platforms are pointing the way to entirely more competent, participatory and trustworthy types of authority systems and institutions. Self-correcting, evolvable institutional designs are starting to provide more effective, adaptive and resilient social and economic institutions. This goal should be the focus of governance design and innovation in the future.

How Does Self-Sovereign Authentication Work?

Let us circle back for a moment to explain the "atomic foundation" upon which the new ODESS services and institutions are based: self-sovereign authentication. As long as some third party – whether it be a state, a bank or a social media site – is the source of an individual's identity credentials, that individual's freedom and control over their identity and personal data are limited. If anything should be inalienable, it should be one's identity – the right to assert and control who you are. Relinquish, delegate or appropriate that control, and what is left but servile dependency.

Yet the big question remains, Can one be self-sovereign? That sounds like a contradiction. How can one have an identity credential issued that is authoritative, independent, incorruptible, and universally accepted by others?

It is vital that no single entity, public or private, should have the power to issue a global identity credential. But who then should vouch for a person's identity if not the state or some "international agency"? That question has been answered convincingly by the universal success of the open source software movement. By combining the norms of autonomy, security and innovation of the open source movement with the transformative powers of ODESS protocols and services, a genuinely new environment for institutional and governance innovation is possible.

The Bitcoin and Ripple algorithms are both open and not owned by anyone, and yet there are also shared protocols that serve as a type of social contract among participants in the system. So it shall be with ODESS platforms and services: algorithms for computing global identities will be open to review and not owned by any party, and self-organized communities will be capable of issuing and enforcing their own identity credentials, independent of states, banks, and other authority institutions. This will enable a whole new class of institutions to self-organize and develop organizational capacities and protections for solutions to fundamental issues of human rights and dignity that previously were simply not conceivable.

Here is how self-sovereign authentication can work: An algorithm would have to compute a unique credential for everyone on the planet based upon something that is uniquely identifying to them. Fortunately, people have many biological and behavioral markers that are unique to them, ranging from how they move or shake a phone, to their daily movements and interactions, to the rhythm and pace of their typing and speaking. All of these markers can be digitally captured. Indeed, with recent advances in genomics, the genome itself is one such "unique identifier" which is digitally captured by default.

While in some cases, a single biological or behavioral marker may not be uniquely identifying, a combination of such markers can produce a unique and distinctive marker. Unlike a fingerprint, retina scan or similar "one time" biological markers that are fixed and therefore potentially appropriated by third parties, these new markers change dynamically over time as the behavior and the biology of the individual changes over time – and they can correspondingly be verified in real time. By having a dynamic and evolving credential that changes with the individual, the resulting credential is not only more credible and perishable, it also makes the individual the living custodian of the credential. As a living credential, it cannot be easily appropriated by someone else and it ceases to be valid when the individual is no longer living. In this sense, it is truly inalienable and is a living digital representation of an individual.

The approach taken here is a variant of forms of security and privacy analyses called L-Diversity, k-Anonymity,[2] Trace analysis[3] and Differential Privacy[4]. In the simplest of terms, the challenge of creating a unique identifier for a person is the inverse of re-identification (determining a person's identity from anonymous data). In the case of geolocation data gleaned from mobile devices, for instance, de Montjoye et al. have found that it takes only four unique coordinates from cellular phone data to identify a person with 95% accuracy.[5] The power of this technique, however, depends upon the density of the populations and groups being analyzed. For instance, if there were few people in sparse locations with few roads, then the opportunity for variability-uniqueness would be more limited, and hence, the "identity distance" between individuals more limited. If on the other hand, it were a highly dense and diverse population with multiple local, regional, national and even international routes, then the opportunity for identity diversity would be significantly greater.

All this suggests that any algorithm based upon movement and interactions would also have to consider not just the size and entropy of the population in which the individual resides or works, but the richness and diversity (entropy) of roads and modes of interaction. This measure could be augmented by adding more signature dimensions in the form of orthogonal behavioral and biological markers – such as, cardiac, gesture, typing, and voice signatures. It is also possible to have a "sliding scale" of credential reliability tied to the level of risk or value in a given transaction. In emerging mobile markets where transaction volumes and amounts are infrequent and under $25 in value, the KYC (Know Your Customer) and AML (Anti-Money Laundering) authentication algorithm could be lighter, but as the volume and amounts of transactions increase, more rigorous credentials and real-time authentication methods could be used.

In the near future it is very likely that many people will have their own sensor platform "bracelets" like the Nike FuelBand, a universal tool for measuring all sorts of a person's activities. These sensor platforms can provide more accurate and unique location, movement and biometric data than phones alone and could be used for more secure forms of authentication and sharing in the near future.

Under any circumstances, an individual's identity signature would be stored in an encrypted personal cloud that could only be accessed through a secure API to upgrade the signature and to allow third-party verification. Moreover, such a root signature could use homographic encryption so that it could be queried without having to be decrypted. It would be from this root signature that a "root" password would be generated by another Open Algorithm, which in turn would generate an OpenID OAuth 2.0 token to create a secure universal password. Should an individual lose or change the password, another could be generated. Since it is generated off the same root identity signature, it could not be "spoofed" because it would be derived from the encrypted root credential that only the individual has access to. This would obviate the problem of individuals forgetting or losing their password and not being able to recover or use their data or a service, because they could easily recover and regenerate a credential based upon their own actions. It may take time for full authentication to take place so there could be a "watch period" until the full richness of the credential is (re)created and verified.

Personas and Contextual Identities

In practice, humans have multiple identities; we are many people to different people; we are parents, spouses, workers, citizens, friends, patients, learners, buyers, makers, etc. Some of these different worlds overlap, but in many cases they do not, and in some cases, it is important that each context *not* be aware of the other or knows everything about the other. This compartmentalization of lives and information is a core component of privacy and essential for both personal and social freedoms.

Such contextual identities we call personas. They are derived from one's root identity but are defined by specific attributes and credentials that are needed to function in those contexts. For example, in a family context, the key attribute is relatedness – parent, child, husband, wife or spouse. These can be biological and socially asserted roles dependent upon specific social conventions and customs. In either case, they cannot be asserted by the individual but need to be asserted and verified by the group defining the context. One person can have many personas, each contextually defined and each wholly independent of the other to the outside world. In some cases, a persona my be legally prescribed by a nation state, such as citizenship and a passport with required picture, certified birth certificate, and residency. In other cases, the persona may be based upon some attributes of mutual interest to everyone in a group or community –

such as age, residency, income, education. Whereas there are many organizations such as banks, credit bureaus, government agencies, schools, health care organizations and the like which claim to be authorities for the verification of certain attributes, such as FICO scores for creditworthiness, many of these services themselves are subject to manipulation.

Open Algorithms for Personas

Again, there is a significant opportunity to have independent and open algorithms to calculate persona *proxy attributes* that can be derived from behavioral and biometric data to verify certain claims about people – such as their residence, employment, creditworthiness, sociality, health, affinities, activities and interest. Such data would be solely under the control of the individual and be shared in their personal cloud or Trusted Compute Cell (TCC). Using the Open Mustard Seed platform (OMS) these personal data could be shared at the discretion of the individual through their own open source Trusted Application Bundles.

Personal Data Assets and Exchanges

If individuals were able to collect and verify their own personal data in their own personal cloud or TCC, then they would have the opportunity to create asset value out of their own personal data. This is a new kind of asset class[6] that has been priced and valued in standard markets such as those formed by data brokers and ad networks. For example, Acxiom, Experian, and Equifax make billion dollar markets in relatively low quality and incomplete data and individuals themselves do not realize value from their own data. Imagine how valuable fully complete, accurate, timely and consensual personal data would be. For the less advantaged individuals, it would be a way of creating social capital and real financial equity for both their data and their actions, and therefore, would be a powerful means for the "unbanked" to bootstrap themselves into a global digital economy.

Through the use of data asset exchanges where individuals and groups could make markets using their data assets, a new business model for web content and services would be possible. Such a business model might well displace the current advertising model where the financial incentives are to trick people out of their data and to push inappropriate offers at people. Imagine a world where people got fair value for their data and would be in charge of how they would be approached by vendors and third parties. That would not only change the "balance of power" between individuals corporations and governments, it would unlock new sources of innovation and greater service efficiencies by making the management of market and security risk based upon more accurate and complete data analytics.

None of this would be possible, however, if individuals were not self-sovereign and in charge of their own identities and personal data. If other parties, governments or corporations, are in charge of the enrollment process, then the old dictum of *Quis custodiet ipsos custodies* would assert itself once again and undermine the very trust and transparency needed to have a free and open digital ecology.

John H. Clippinger *is co-founder and Executive Director of ID3 (Institute for Innovation & Data Driven Design), a nonprofit organization formed to develop and field test legal and software trust frameworks for data-driven services, infrastructures and enterprises. He is also Research Scientist at the M.I.T. Media Lab's Human Dynamics Group. Previously, Dr. Clippinger was founder and Co-Director of The Law Lab at the Berkman Center for Internet & Society at Harvard University. He is the author of* A Crowd of One: The Future of Individual Identity *(2007) and* The Biology of Business *(1998).*

Notes

[1] Bollier, David and John H. Clippinger, "The Next Great Internet Disruption: Authority and Governance," available at http://idcubed.org/?post_type=home_page_feature&p=631. See also Clippinger, John H., *A Crowd of One, The Future of Individual Identity* (Public Affairs, 2007).

[2] Machanavajjhala, A., Kifer, D., Gehrke, J., and Venkitasubramaniam, M., "Diversity: Privacy Beyond k-Anonymity," *ACM Trans. Knowl. Discov. Data* 1, 1, Article 3 (March 2007) [DOI=10.1145/1217299.1217302], available at http://doi.acm.org/10.1145/1217299.1217302; see also Lantanya Sweeney, "k-Anonymity: A Model for Protecting Privacy," *International Journal on Uncertainty, Fuzziness and Knowledge-based Systems*, 10 (5) (2002), pp. 557–570, available at http://dataprivacylab.org/dataprivacy/projects/kanonymity/kanonymity.pdf.

[3] Yves-Alexandre de Montjoye, César A. Hidalgo, Michel Verleysen and Vincent D. Blondel, "Unique in the Crowd: The Privacy Bounds of Human Mobility," *Nature* (March 2013); and Lantanya Sweeney, "Uniqueness of Simple Demograph-

ics in the U.S. Population," Technical Report LIDAP-WP4 (Pittsburgh, Pa.: Carnegie Mellon University, 2000), available at http://dataprivacylab.org/projects/identifiability/index.html.

[4] Ninghui Li, Wahbeh Qardaji, Dong Su, "Provably Private Data Anonymization: Or, K-Anonymity Meets Differential Privacy," *CERIAS Tech Report 2010-27*, Center for Education and Research, Information Assurance and Security (West Lafayette, Indiana: Purdue University, 2010).

[5] Yves-Alexandre de Montjoye, César A. Hidalgo, Michel Verleysen & Vincent D. Blondel, "Unique in the Crowd: The Privacy Bounds of Human Mobility." *Nature*, (March 2013).

[6] World Economic Forum, *Personal Data: The Emergence of a New Asset Class* (2011).

Chapter 3

The Next Great Internet Disruption: Authority and Governance

By David Bollier and John H. Clippinger

As the Internet and digital technologies have proliferated over the past twenty years, incumbent enterprises nearly always resist open network dynamics with fierce determination, a narrow ingenuity and resistance. It arguably started with AOL (vs. the Web and browsers), Lotus Notes (vs. the Web and browsers) and Microsoft MSN (vs. the Web and browsers, Amazon in books and eventually everything) before moving on to the newspaper industry (Craigslist, blogs, news aggregators, podcasts), the music industry (MP3s, streaming, digital sales, video through streaming and YouTube), and telecommunications (VoIP, WiFi). But the inevitable rearguard actions to defend old forms are invariably overwhelmed by the new, network-based ones. The old business models, organizational structures, professional sinecures, cultural norms, etc., ultimately yield to open platforms.

When we look back on the past twenty years of Internet history, we can more fully appreciate the prescience of David P. Reed's seminal 1999 paper on "Group Forming Networks" (GFNs).[1] "Reed's Law" posits that value in networks increases exponentially as interactions move from a *broadcasting* model that offers "best content" (in which value is described by n, the number of consumers) to a network of *peer-to-peer transactions* (where the network's value is based on "most members" and mathematically described by n^2). But by far the most valuable networks are based on those that *facilitate group affiliations*, Reed concluded. When users have tools for "free and responsible association for common purposes," he found, the value of the network soars exponentially to 2^n – a fantastically large number.

This is the *Group Forming Network*. Reed predicted that "the dominant value in a typical network tends to shift from one category to another as the scale of the network increases...."

What is really interesting about Reed's analysis is that today's world of GFNs, as embodied by Facebook, Twitter, Wikipedia and other Web 2.0 technologies, remains highly rudimentary. It is based on proprietary platforms (as opposed to open source, user-controlled platforms), and therefore provides only limited tools for members of groups to develop trust and confidence in each other. This suggests a huge, unmet opportunity to actualize greater value from open networks. Citing Francis Fukuyama's book *Trust*, Reed points out that "there is a strong correlation between the prosperity of national economies and *social* capital, which [Fukuyama] defines culturally as the ease with which people in a particular culture can form new associations."

A Network Architecture for Group Forming Networks

If we take Reed's analysis of network dynamics seriously, and apply his logic to the contemporary scene, it becomes clear that the best way to unlock enormous stores of value on networks is to develop tools that can facilitate GFNs. This will be the next great Internet disruption. But to achieve this, we must develop a network architecture and software systems that can enable people to build trust and social capital in user-centric, scalable ways.

Necessarily, this means that we must begin to re-imagine the very nature of authority and governance. We must invent new types of digital institutions that are capable of administering authority recognized as authentic and use algorithmic tools to craft and enforce "law."

The idea that conventional institutions of governance (and government) may have to change may seem like a far-fetched idea. Who dares to question the venerable system of American government? Traditions are deeply rooted and seemingly rock-solid. But why should government be somehow immune from the same forces that have disrupted Encyclopedia Britannica, retailing in all sectors, the music industry, metropolitan daily newspapers and book publishing? Based on existing trends, we believe the next wave of Internet disruptions is going to redefine the nature of authority and governance. It is going to transform existing institutions of law and create new types of legal institutions – "code as law," as Lawrence Lessig famously put it.

Governance is about legitimate authority making decisions that are respected by members of a given community. These decisions generally allocate rights of access and usage of resources, among other rights and privileges. Such governance generally requires a capacity to assert and validate who we are – to determine our identity in one aspect or another. That's what is happening when the state issues us birth certificates, passports, Social Security numbers and drivers' licenses. It is assigning us identities that come with certain privileges, duties and sanctions. This is the prerogative of institutions of governance – the ability to do things *to you* and *for you*. Institutions set criteria for our entitlements to certain civic, political, economic and cultural benefits. In the case of religious institutions, such authority even extends to the afterlife!

The power to govern is often asserted, but it may or may not be based on authentic social consent. This is an important issue because open networks are changing the nature of legitimate authority and the consent of the governed. User communities are increasingly asserting their own authority, assigning identities to people, and allocating rights and privileges in the manner of any conventional institution. Anonymous, Five Star Movement, the Pirate Party, Arab Spring, Lulzsec and Occupy are notable examples of such grassroots, network-enabled movements – and there are plenty of other instances in which distributed networks of users work together toward shared goals in loosely coordinated, bottom-up ways. Such "smart mobs" – elementary forms of GFNs – are showing that they have the legitimacy and legal authority and the economic and cultural power to act as "institutions" with a modicum of governance power.

This is where Reed's Law and the proliferation of open networks, amplified by the ubiquity of mobile devices, is starting to make things very interesting. If the means to facilitate GFNs can be taken to more secure and trusted levels, empowering cooperative action on larger scales, it opens up a vast new realm of opportunity for value-creation above and beyond Web 2.0 platforms.

This vision is especially attractive in light of the structural limitations of large, centralized institutions of government and commerce. By virtue of their (antiquated) design, they simply are not capable of solving the challenges we are demanding of them. Conventional legislation, regulations and litigation are simply too crude and unresponsive to provide governance that is seen as legitimate and responsive. As for social networking platforms, they typically rely upon proprietary business models that collect and sell personal information about users, which is exposing another sort of structural barrier: social distrust. Businesses based on such revenue-models cannot help but stifle the GFN potential described by Reed's Law.

Group Forming Networks and Big Data

The promise of self-organized network governance – a new type of Group Forming Network – holds a great deal of appeal when it comes to Big Data. We now live in a world of ubiquitous digital networks and databases that contain vast amounts of personal information about individuals. GFNs could help us overcome the legal and regulatory impasse that we now face with respect to the management of such personal data. Neither Congress, executive agencies nor the courts are likely to come up with a set of responsive policies that can keep pace with technological innovation and thwart players of ill-intent.

Ever since Hobbes proposed the State as the only viable alternative to the dread state of nature, citizens have entered into a notional "social contract" with "the Leviathan" to protect their safety and basic rights. But if networked technologies could enable individuals to negotiate their own social contract(s) and meet their needs more directly and responsively, it would enable the emergence of new sorts of effective, quasi-autonomous governance and self-provisioning. And it could achieve these goals without necessarily or directly requiring government. Online communities working in well-designed software environments could act more rapidly, with highly specific knowledge and with greater social legitimacy than conventional government institutions. Users, acting individually and in groups, could use their own secure digital identities to manage their own personal information.

This scenario is inspired not just by David Reed's analysis of how to reap value from networks, but by the extensive scholarship of Professor Elinor Ostrom, the Nobel Laureate in economics in 2009. Ostrom identified key principles by which self-organized groups can manage common-pool resources in fair, sustainable ways. If data were to be regarded as a common-pool resource, Ostrom's research shows how it would be possible for online groups to devise their own *data commons* to manage their personal data in their own interests. (For more, see Chapter 12, "The Algorithmic Governance of Common-Pool Resources," by Jeremy Pitt and Ada Diaconescu.)

Of course, "law" emerging from self-organized digital institutions would have a very different character than the kinds of law emanating from Congress and the Supreme Court (just as blogging is a different from journalism and Wikipedia is different from Encyclopedia Britannica). "Digital law" would be algorithmic in the sense that machine-learning would help formulate and administer the law and enforce compliance. It would enable users to devise new types of legal contracts that are computationally expressible and executable, as well as evolvable and auditable. Such an innovation would make institutional corruption and insider collusion far easier to detect and eliminate. Arcane systems of law – once based on oral traditions and printed texts – could make the great leap to computable code, providing powerful new platforms for governance. Law that is dynamic, evolvable and outcome-oriented would make the art of governance subject to the iterative innovations of Moore's Law. Designs could be experimentally tested, evaluated by actual outcomes, and made into better iterations.

Open Mustard Seed

Mindful of the functional limits of conventional government and policymaking – and of the unmet promise of Reed's Law despite the ubiquity of the Internet – it is time to take fuller advantage of the versatile value-generating capacities of open network platforms. It is time to develop new sorts of network-native institutions of law and governance. That is the frank ambition of the new software platform Open Mustard Seed (OMS), which seeks to enable users to build new sorts of decentralized, dynamically responsive and transparent digital institutions. By enabling people to build trust and cooperation among each other, Open Mustard Seed seeks to fulfill the promise of Reed's Law. (For more on OMS, see Chapter 13, "The ID3 Open Mustard Seed Platform," by Thomas Hardjono, Patrick Deegan and John H. Clippinger, and Chapter 14, "The Relational Matrix," by Patrick Deegan.)

OMS provides a new infrastructure to let people build their own highly distributed social ecosystems for reliably governing all sorts of shared resources, including their personal data. The software is a synthesis of a variety of existing software systems – for digital identity, security, computable legal contracts and data-management – designed to serve as a new platform for social exchange and online governance. Just as the original html code gave rise to the World Wide Web and new types of bottom-up social communication and collaboration, OMS can be conceived as a new "social stack" of protocols and software for self-organized governance. Instead of looking to (unreliable, unwieldy) external institutions of law and policy, OMS uses software code to *internalize governance* to individuals and online communities.

OMS solves a number of interrelated problems about Big Data. Users have not had an easy or reliable means to express their preferences for how their personal data may be accessed and used, especially when one context (a bank) differs so much from another (a healthcare provider) and still others (family and friends). A user may not know with whom they are really transacting, nor can they readily verify that their privacy preferences are actually respected and enforced. Users are often wary of exposing or sharing their data with third parties whose trustworthiness is not known. In this context, it is not surprising that protecting one's personal information is seen as antithetical to commercial and governmental uses of it.

The Open Mustard Seed project seeks to overcome these problems through a technical architecture called the "Trusted Compute

Framework" (TCF). The TCF extends the core functionality of "Personal Data Stores" (PDS) – digital repositories in the cloud that let users strictly control their personal information – by enabling online users to interact flexibly with third parties in secure, trustworthy ways.

In such a network environment, one can imagine an ecosystem of "branded portals" emerging as central repositories for people's personal data. One can also imagine companies arising to serve as "trust providers" of social, secure, cloud-based applications. Users could begin to enjoy many benefits that stem from sharing their data (avoidance of advertising, group discounts, trusted interactions with affinity groups and strangers, etc.) Businesses that engage with this architecture (app developers, service providers, retailers) could gain trusted access to large, highly refined pools of personal data that can be monetized directly or indirectly, using new business models. Government institutions, similarly, could gain access to large pools of personal data without violating people's privacy or the Fourth Amendment, and craft more reliable, effective and demographically refined policies and programs. As a completely decentralized and open source platform, OMS cannot be "captured" by any single player or group. It aims to be always capable of the kinds of open-ended innovation that we have seen in open source software, the Web and other open platforms.

The Future of Governance

The OMS platform has sweeping implications for political governance in both theoretical and practical terms. It could transform the role of the State by empowering citizens to devise new forms of self-actualized institutions. These institutions would likely provide greater social legitimacy, efficacy and adaptability than conventional government. Instead of regarding political authority as something inherent in government and law, OMS seeks to ratify a deeper social reality – that authority is a *collective social process* that arises through the autonomous expressions of a group's needs, values and commitments. Legitimate authority is ultimately vested in a community's ongoing, evolving social life, and not in ritualistic forms of citizenship. Any new GFN software will clearly need to undergo refinement and evolution in the coming years. Yet Reed's Law suggests that this is the inevitable trajectory of the Internet and the economic and social changes that it is driving. We should embrace this future because it offers us a compelling pathway for moving beyond the many deep structural impasses in our troubled system of government, politics, economy and culture.

David Bollier *is Editor at ID3 and an author, blogger and independent scholar/activist who is the author of twelve books, most recently* Think Like a Commoner *and* Green Governance. *He cofounded the Commons Strategies Group in 2010 and the Washington, D.C., policy advocacy group Public Knowledge in 2002.*

John H. Clippinger *is cofounder and Executive Director of ID3 (Institute for Institutional Innovation by Data-Driven Design), a nonprofit organization formed to develop and field test legal and software trust frameworks for data-driven services, infrastructures, and enterprises. He is also Research Scientist at the M.I.T. Media Lab's Human Dynamics Group. Previously, Dr. Clippinger was founder and Co-Director of The Law Lab at the Berkman Center for Internet & Society at Harvard University. He is the author of* A Crowd of One: The Future of Individual Identity *(2007) and* The Biology of Business *(1998).*

References
[1] David P. Reed, "The Sneaky Exponential – Beyond Metcalfe's Law to the Power of Community Building," at http://www.reed.com/dpr/locus/gfn/reedslaw.html.

Chapter 4

The New Mestieri Culture of Artisans

By Maurizio Rossi

IF THERE IS ONE KEY LESSON to be learned from the Internet, it is that we are moving from an "Industrial Age" to an "Entrepreneurial Age," a paradigm shift in how we design, produce, manufacture and market products. Historically, human beings have adapted to new technologies; increasingly, however, we are moving to a world where new technologies will adapt to individual human needs and behaviors.

In the new environment of open networks and fluid knowledge-sharing, the most competitive companies will not survive as closed, proprietary systems working in vertical value-chains. They will constantly need to leverage people's creativity, spontaneity, serendipity, knowledge and passion. This type of engagement will extend not just to a company's staff and suppliers, but to customers and the general public.

These organizational shifts are necessary because technologies are empowering collaboration on a much larger scale, making it a routine fact of life. This is fostering a new emphasis on *relational* patterns in business instead of simply *transactional* ones. Each individual is becoming a peer in a larger community – a personal producer and entrepreneur who uses a variety of platforms to carry on a variety of relationships – not just among humans, but with machines. This environment of hyper-connectivity and relationships is empowering people to produce, design or service almost anything.

In my country, Italy, many industries are rooted in old artisan cultures called "Mestieri." Some of them have grown and adapted to the industrial age, earning a solid reputation for their craftsmanship. Their commitment to artisanship and high quality work remains a deep part of their organizational culture even as industrial production has become the norm. Mass-market production simply cannot match the quality of such artisanal enterprises.

But the pervasive role of the Internet and other digital technologies in mainstream commerce is changing this equation. I believe that we are at the beginning of the "New Artisan" generation, in which skilled workers – often, young people – will be able to combine deep knowledge and experience in a given field of artisanship with new technologies such as 3D printing, robotics, artificial intelligence and "smart materials." We are seeing the digital mindset blend with artisanal culture, and we are seeing the rise of new business models that make artisanal quality products widely accessible, profitable and scalable.

This will change the commercial landscape significantly, and it will open up a completely new spectrum of challenges. When the boundaries between a company and its partners, suppliers, customers and future staff become blurry and porous, a company needs to re-think how it will manage those relationships over the long term. I believe that competitive companies will need to develop entirely new "relational structures" – for educating and recruiting new talent, for securing the attention and loyalty of customers, and for managing production in an always-changing "value network" (rather than static, linear "value chains").

We can already see hints of this future in the advertising industry with Web-based innovators like Zooppa. Zooppa has attracted more than 243,000 creatives to come up with crowd-created and -critiqued advertising campaigns. The giant, traditional advertising firms regard Zooppa as a novelty and perhaps as a niche competitor. They do not understand that it represents a transformative model for advertising that is likely to expand in coming years – a model based on radically dynamic social interaction. Advertising as a social conversation.

Incumbent industry leaders always seem to have this problem: they see upstart innovators through the lens of existing markets. Hence Zooppa is seen as "just another advertising firm." In truth, Zooppa is a new socially based, rapid-response platform for building trust and credibility in a brand. It is about redefining the very meaning of "branding" and the social framework for marketing.

Camera makers had a similar blind spot when smartphones started to include simple cameras. The photography world was condescending to this innovation and did not see it as a serious threat. But over time the quality of smartphone cameras got a lot better, and soon smartphones began siphoning away business from traditional camera-makers.

We can see a similar response to Nest, the innovative "smart thermostat" that incumbent manufacturers failed to see as a serious competitor. Nest was seen as a niche novelty – a Wi-Fi-enabled, auto-scheduling thermostat that can be remotely controlled from a smartphone or laptop. Now that Nest has been acquired by Google, it is more evident that thermostats are not just themostats any more. They should be seen as a powerful point of access to a wider universe of digital devices and cloud services.

It is noteworthy that the innovators mentioned here emerged from the periphery of established markets. Historically, the dominant businesses in an industry could safely ignore the edge because – even though great ideas sometime arose there – they could not easily scale. Artisanal culture was permanently consigned to the fringe. The quality and customization that were born in small shops and local industries could not reach global markets nor maintain their quality standards if they tried.

But that is changing today. Artisanal production and culture can increasingly reach consumers and scale rapidly. We see this every day among Internet startups, which grow from a few programmers to very large enterprises in only a few years.

Now imagine this dynamic playing out in markets based on physical production, such as the design, manufacturing and retailing of countless everyday products. Large, brand-name manufacturers and retail chains are going to face increasingly fierce pressures from small, artisan-based companies. Why? Because those companies will be able to deliver stylish, customized products at any location, on demand. They will go beyond the impersonal, one-size-fits-all feel of mass-produced products, and instead conform to the social attitudes, needs and practices of small and localized niches of consumers.

Mass-market manufacturers will also need to rethink their production processes.

For decades, large companies have sought out low-wage countries to produce their products, which are then shipped halfway across the world to reach customers at a retail outlet. As Apple advertises, "Designed in California" – while its products are quietly, without fanfare, produced in China.

This design and production model will face new pressures as the artisanal business culture develops the capacity to out-compete the historic model. Experienced craftspeople in one location – say, Italy – will increasingly be able to sell products that are manufactured on-demand at thousands of retail locations around the world. The special design and production knowledge that a local community of artisans have cultivated, will be able to be transmitted to 3D printers in thousands of retail stores, for example. A Long Tail of distinctive, high-quality eyewear will be available on a mass-market basis. One company that I know envisions producing ten new models every day.

The artisan-driven model will become supremely efficient, not to mention customer-friendly, because its design, production and retailing will take advantage of the modularity made possible by open networks. This is how the Web functions, and why all sorts of startups have been able to disintermediate large, well-established industries. In the near future, large companies with static, vertical supply chains will find themselves at a disadvantage in competing against artisanal suppliers who have greater speed, flexibility, social connections to customers and creativity.

We are going to see new ways of conceiving, designing, marketing and retailing products. Production and manufacturing of products will be diffused rather than concentrated, as in the industrial model. Groups of artisans will participate in larger manufacturing networks that are able to participate on shared platforms, much as APIs provide a point of access to shared technology platforms for Apple and Amazon.

Branding itself will undergo a transformation. Instead of closed, proprietary brands that peddle an unattainable dream, image or life-style, brands will become "open." That is, many artisans and companies will contribute to the brand identity and image. The brand will not be a proprietary, top-down creation "owned" by a single company; it will be a bottom-up social enactment that "belongs" to the collaborative community of artisans, companies, suppliers and customers, all of whom participate in the shared ecosystem. Open brands will have a social authenticity – a credibility and depth – that is rarely associated with branded products today.

The closest version of open branding today would be the social ecosystems that revolve around software platforms such as Linux and Apache, and around the open hardware world known as Arduino. Participation in a branded ecosystem is available to anyone, but participation is predicated on accepting certain principles, protocols and behaviors.

While conventional companies would probably be threatened by the idea of other businesses "participating" in "their" brands, open branding simply reflects the new realities of ubiquitous open networks – and then leverages it. After all, any company is embedded in a complex cluster of interdependencies. Why not make the most of that? Instead of trying to "go it alone" in the style of traditional, proprietary business models, open branding enlists all participants in a shared ecosystem to cooperate (in building the brand) while competing (on the basis of a distinctive value-added).

This new understanding of brands is more realistic than industrial-era branding because it recognizes that brands are not idealized, remote icons, but rather living, breathing social systems. Open brands provide a way for artisanal enterprises and their suppliers and customers to collectively express a shared commitment to certain standards of quality, production ethics and community values.

Mestieri-based branding will establish strong, credible linkages between artisan-producers and customers via API-based platforms for design, production and retail. Designers will be able to instill their authentic, distinctive craftsmanship into products, and highly distributed local manufacturing outlets around the world will be able to deliver higher quality products. Customers will enjoy the conveniences of vast choice, on-demand production, customized features and express delivery – and companies will avoid the inefficiencies, limited choices and unsold inventories that plague conventional production.

Of course, many questions remain unanswered. How shall the new generation of artisans learn and cultivate their skills? How can artisanal companies develop the brand relationships with customers and fend off takeovers by large companies that wish to stifle the competitive alternatives that they offer?

To be sure, incumbent market players, especially large companies invested in old infrastructures and business models, will resist this new world. That is always the case when disruptive innovation arises. And startups will need to be savvy in maintaining their integrity of vision, especially since large companies will find it convenient to buy startups as a way to learn new tricks.

But we have seen how each new generation of tech innovators always has some determined visionaries eager to break with the old ways and forge new paths that are both profitable and socially appealing. These challenges will be made easier by the proliferation of "out of control" technologies that can work on open digital networks.

Artisanal production will not supplant everything else. There will still be large manufacturing concerns based on economies of scale. But they will coexist with – and be challenged by – networks of smaller companies and solo businesses that can compete with greater agility, speed and customization.

The new production capabilities will post a clear challenge to traditional consumer culture, however. For years, manufacturers have cultivated a strict dichotomy between low quality/low price and prestigious brands/high price (but not necessarily high quality/high price). The challenge going forward will be to validate the market position of higher quality/higher price products (but not luxury, not Cucinelli's). This will not be a trivial challenge.

The transition will also require visionary entrepreneurs who are willing to understand the new technologies and master the artisanal skills to shape new commercial models. These leaders must have a commitment to quality and taste, and recognize that redefining mainstream consumer expectations will take time. Within their companies, too, they will need to develop new forms of apprenticeships and education to nourish artisanal cultures, especially as existing masters of various crafts grow older.

Finally, the rise of the Mestieri production culture will require appropriate frameworks of applications. Mainstream social networks today are still mostly used for entertainment. While there are a number of game-changing platforms for crowdsourcing and crowdfunding, these applications will need to expand and become more versatile if they are to become engines for digital artisans.

Many unresolved issues will need to be addressed, obviously, but it is clear that as the company of tomorrow moves to open platforms, traditional linear chains of production developed in the industrial era will give way to loose networks of designers, producers and customers. And this will require that we understand production as far more than a transactional process, and more as a deeply relational one.

Maurizio Rossi started his business career in sales and new market development for Rossimoda, a leading Italian luxury footwear company started by his grandfather. In the early 1990s, Rossi started a new sports apparel business division, Vista Point, whose brands he licensed and distributed globally for over ten years. Rossimoda was later acquired by the luxury giant LVMH. In 2005, Rossi cofounded H-FARM, a platform for incubating a new generation of Italian entrepreneurs.

Chapter 5

Burning Man:
The Pop-Up City of Self-Governing Individualists

By Peter Hirshberg

WHEN FRIENDS FIRST STARTED TELLING ME about Burning Man in the 1990s it made me nervous. This place in a harsh desert, where they wore strange clothes or perhaps none at all. Why? Whole swaths of my San Francisco community spent much of the year building massive works of art or collaborating on elaborate camps where they had to provide for every necessity. They were going to a place with no water, no electricity, no shade and no shelter. And they were completely passionate about going to this place to create a city out of nothing. To create a world they imagined – out of nothing. A world with rules, mores, traditions and principles, which they more or less made up, and then lived.

Twenty-eight years later Burning Man has emerged as a unique canvas on which to run city-scale experiments. It attracts some of the most creative and accomplished people on the planet. It's big. Sixty-eight thousand people attended in 2013. It inspires broad-based participation, imagination and play. It pushes our thinking about society: Can anyone really imagine an economy based on gifts and generosity, not on monetary transactions? If only for a week, Burning Man is a place where art, performance and radical self-expression are the most valued activities of a society. It is a place apart, with the least government and the most freedom of any place I can think of on earth. Where thousands of people self-organize into theme camps, art projects, pulsing sound villages, fire-dancing troupes, groups of performers, a department of public works, rangers to patrol the site, and a temporary airport.

Because Burning Man is a phantasmagoria of possibility, a completely dreamed-up city built from scratch each year, it's an opportunity to relax the constraints of your world, your job and your imagined "role" in the world. As Burning Man founder Larry Harvey points out, "It's about personal agency. It's about being able to create the world you live in. We make the world real through actions that open the heart."

At a time when people don't trust institutions as we once did, when what bubbles up is a lot more attractive than what trickles down, Burning Man is a fascinating place to observe the large-scale practice of self-organizing governance in action. Its quarter century history lets us look back and see what worked and what didn't. We can see which strains of political and organizational thought and city design have endured and which were cast aside. In Burning Man we can observe the constant tension between centralized organization and emergent activity on the edge. It is a lab for testing the balance of extreme liberty and community – or, to quote its self-described principles, between "radical self-expression" and "radical self-reliance" on the one hand, and "radical inclusion," "civic responsibility" and "communal effort" on the other.

Burning Man is self-organized by thousands of people and camps from all over the world, but its core directions are set by a small team of founders who curate and exercise their judgment more as Plato's philosopher-king than as leaders of a democratic state. They set the size of Burning Man, negotiate with state and federal agencies for land access rights, design the contours of the city, sell tickets, provide grants to select artists, and create a framework for education and communication for the global Burning Man community. The dialogue among participants and with the founders brings to mind Publius, author of the Federalist Papers, who argued with his peers about the proper governance principles for a new social order. The difference is that Burning Man is undertaking this inquiry as an ever-changing experiment in a swirl of costumes and music on a remote, antediluvian dried salt lakebed.

Some basic facts: Burning Man is an annual week-long event held in Nevada's Black Rock desert. It is one of the most God-forsaken environments in North America – a vast semi-arid desert with lava beds and alkali flats. Amidst 380,000 acres of wilderness arises Black Rock City, the seven-square mile temporary city that is Burning Man. When it's over, everything is gone, without a trace. Burning Man's arrangement with the U.S. Bureau of Land Management, from which it leases the land, is that nothing be left behind—not a piece of paper, a shoe, a sequin.[1]

That is part of Burning Man's philosophy of radical self -reliance. You build this city as a participant, and then pack everything out. (A subtle cue: Burning Man sets out no garbage cans in its city, a reminder you'll have to handle that problem on your own.) There is no government to come clean up after you, and no one to provide lighting or a power grid. You, your friends, your camp have to solve these problems yourselves. This forces you to think about systems, resource sharing, and new approaches to self-organizing. And while the event is temporary, the experience and its insights linger long afterwards, both because the Burner community (as they call themselves) is often engaged in planning all year long, and because this freed-up way of thinking has a way of influencing peoples lives, careers, projects and civic engagement long after everyone packs up and leaves the desert.

It is said of Burning Man that people come for the art and stay for the community. In my own case, the overwhelming impression when I first arrived in 2005 was of miles and miles of fantastic vehicles and structures ringing the central core of Burning Man and extending deep into the *playa* – "beach" in Spanish. People spend countless hours creating strange vehicles and "buildings": a vehicle resembling a giant octopus with fire-spouting tentacles....a half-sunk pirate ship rising out of the desert with its sixty-foot mast....a small-town church leaping at an angle from the ground, organ blasting.

At the center of it all is The Man – a nearly hundred-foot-tall sculpture that serves as an anchor point for the city until it is burned on the penultimate night of the event. Just as the World Trade Center towers once helped New Yorkers locate themselves in Manhattan, the Man provides an orientation point in the desert.

Burning Man has the scale and spectacle of a World's Fair, except that it's not built by companies and countries. It's built by everybody. Participation is one of the core principles of Burning Man, a belief that transformative change occurs through deeply personal involvement. This harkens back to the American tradition of barn-raising where everyone pitches in to help a farmer build his necessary structures; or to Habitat for Humanity, where the entire community is involved in building homes for those who need them.

Urbanist Jane Jacobs, in her classic book *The Death and Life of Great American Cities*, understood the importance of this idea when she wrote, "Cities have the capability of providing something for everybody, only because, and only when, they are created by everybody." She was speaking in the context of 1960s urban renewal where city governments tried to build neighborhoods to serve residents, but without engaging them. At Burning Man, the obverse principle is honored: when you participate in building your world you are more engaged and have a sense of agency you'd never have otherwise. Jacobs would also have understood Burning Man's wonderful weirdness. In 1961 she also wrote, " By its nature, the metropolis provides what otherwise could be given only by traveling; namely, the strange."

While Burning Man is fantastic, it embodies many deeply rooted American values. It is Tocquevillian at its core – a great coming together of the most heterodox assemblage of voluntary associations, working in various groups, yet building a network of social trust in a shared city. "Association is the mother of science," said Tocqueville. "The progress of all the rest depends upon the progress it has made." At a time when Americans are accused of spending less time on genuine communities, Burning Man is an intensely purposeful community, a dazzling display of social capital.

From afar it may seem as if Burning Man is a magical, spontaneous creation. In fact, Burning Man works only because there is a core set of shared principles that are almost universally agreed to and self-enforced by the community. Which in turn yields the least amount of government and the most amount of freedom. The dynamics of self-organized governance are remarkably similar to those identified by the late Elinor Ostrom – the Nobel Prize Laureate in economics in 2009 – who spent decades studying the design principles of successful commons. To manage a "common-pool resource" such as a seven-square mile piece of desert with 68,000 inhabitants in 2013, the Burners realize that they are part of a conscious community. Everyone therefore shares responsibility for monitoring each other and enforcing the rules.

In 2004 Larry Harvey published the "Ten Principles of Burning Man" to serve as guidelines for the community. As I work with cities around the world on innovation and fostering creative and maker economies, I find these are broadly applicable guidelines for conceptualizing a more sustainable, more conscious and less materialist world. They make you more self-aware of the personal commitments needed to make a great city work well.

Four of the principles are concerned with how the individual can live a more present, conscious and engaged life: Radical-Self Expression, Radical Self-Reliance, Immediacy, and Participation. Four focus on the community: Communal effort, Civic engagement, Radical Inclusion and Leave No Trace. And the final two are perhaps the most remarkable of all: Gifting and Decommodification. Burning Man's gift economy celebrates the unrequited joy of giving. It's not barter because nothing is expected in return. To keep Burning Man a celebration of the efforts of its participants, there are no brands, no sponsors, no advertising. These are the conditions for a very different, more creative world, yet reminiscent of Aristotle's vision that a good society is built on the transcendental values of truth, goodness and beauty – the core of its culture.

The Ten Principles of Burning Man

Radical Inclusion. Anyone may be a part of Burning Man. We welcome and respect the stranger. No prerequisites exist for participation in our community.

Gifting. Burning Man is devoted to acts of gift giving. The value of a gift is unconditional. Gifting does not contemplate a return or an exchange for something of equal value.

Decommodification. In order to preserve the spirit of gifting, our community seeks to create social environments that are unmediated by commercial sponsorships, transactions or advertising. We stand ready to protect our culture from such exploitation. We resist the substitution of consumption for participatory experience.

Radical Self-reliance. Burning Man encourages the individual to discover, exercise and rely on his or her inner resources.

Radical Self-expression. Radical self-expression arises from the unique gifts of the individual. No one other than the individual or a collaborating group can determine its content. It is offered as a gift to others. In this spirit, the giver should respect the rights and liberties of the recipient.

Communal Effort. Our community values creative cooperation and collaboration. We strive to produce, promote and protect social networks, public spaces, works of art, and methods of communication that support such interaction.

Civic Responsibility. We value civil society. Community members who organize events should assume responsibility for public welfare and endeavor to communicate civic responsibilities to participants. They must also assume responsibility for conducting events in accordance with local, state and federal laws.

Leaving No Trace. Our community respects the environment. We are committed to leaving no physical trace of our activities wherever we gather. We clean up after ourselves and endeavor, whenever possible, to leave such places in a better state than when we found them.

Participation. Our community is committed to a radically participatory ethic. We believe that transformative change, whether in the individual or in society, can occur only through the medium of deeply personal participation. We achieve being through doing. Everyone is invited to work. Everyone is invited to play. We make the world real through actions that open the heart.

Immediacy. Immediate experience is, in many ways, the most important touchstone of value in our culture. We seek to overcome barriers that stand between us and a recognition of our inner selves, the reality of those around us, participation in society, and contact with a natural world exceeding human powers. No idea can substitute for this experience.

Today Burning Man has a global reach, with attendees from over two hundred cities and sixty-five officially affiliated events. The global influence of Burning Man stems from its large network of volunteers. For years members of the regional Burning communities have come to San Francisco for an annual conference to learn the skills of business management, fundraising for art, permit-getting, and how-to knowledge-exchange. Two years ago Burning Man reframed that gathering as "The Burning Man Global Leadership Conference." It saw its network not just as people who helped put on Burning Man, but as a global volunteer workforce that could bring Burning Man's can-do problem-solving and community-oriented work to the world.

The whole point of Burning Man, says founder Larry Harvey, is to create the world that you want to live in. We go through life operating under a defined set of rules and roles. We follow a prescribed job. We exist in a prescribed city. "Here, you get to try things you might never have tried before."[2] The stories of people who go to Burning Man are often the stories of personal transition and transformation. When my friend Steve Brown made a film about Burning Man, for example, he found that all of his characters were going through some transition. Katie, an artist, quit her job as a nanny to pursue her artistic passions. Casey Fenton came up with the idea of CouchSurfing, one of the first great projects of the "sharing economy."

Larry Harvey and the Origins of Burning Man

The Burning Man of today wasn't always a hotbed of experimentation, irreverence and community making. In 1986, Larry Harvey started Burning Man as a modest summer-solstice fire party on Baker Beach in San Francisco. Two groups were especially influential in shaping the early Burning Man culture – the followers of anarchist Hakim Bey and the San Francisco Cacophony Society.

Bey's 1991 book, *Temporary Autonomous Zones,* is a manifesto for radical thinkers urging them to live authentically, in the present, and with complete self-expression. But to do so, said Bey, you must disengage from corporate and government authority – and not just theoretically or in your head, but in real physical space.[3] Bey suggested that there is an alternative world – a "temporary autonomous zone," or T.A.Z. – where, under the right conditions, you can create yourself. One of the best descriptions of this social phenomenon is in *Beautiful Trouble,* a contemporary manual for artists and activists that pays homage to Bey:

A T.A.Z. is a liberated area "of land, time or imagination" where one can be for something, not just against, and where new ways of being human together can be explored and experimented with. Locating itself in the cracks and fault lines in the global grid of control and alienation, a T.A.Z. is an eruption of free culture where life is experienced at maximum intensity. It should feel like an exceptional party where for a brief moment our desires are made manifest and we all become the creators of the art of everyday life.[4]

Bey's idea of a T.A.Z. – published about the same time that Tim Berners-Lee was inventing the World Wide Web, but before it became a mass medium – was highly prescient. Bey anticipated by two decades a world of mobile everything – distributed computing, open source software, weak-tie enabled networks, social networking and distributed systems like Bitcoin and Open Mustard Seed. Bey's work seems like a manifesto for creative hacking – a way to prototype fanciful (and not so fanciful) alternatives to oppressive institutions. The idea of a T.A.Z. screams, "You've got permission, so use it!"

At the time Bey was writing, the San Francisco Cacophony Society was enacting many of the same ideas – creating street performances, jamming culture, and showing up at events in costumes. Cacophony members started attending Burning Man when it was still a party on Baker Beach. By 1993, after seven annual parties, Burning Man was finally evicted from the beach because it had grown too big and couldn't secure the necessary permits. It was the Cacophony Society that invited Burning Man to undertake a "zone trip," an extended event that takes participants outside of their local frames of reference.

And so it came to pass that Burning Man, the Cacophony Society, and Bay Area anarchists all headed for the Black Rock desert, in Nevada, to reset Burning Man.

Although Burning Man had not been founded with any subversive or transgressive agenda, it quickly veered in that direction. In the words of founder Larry Harvey, "We were not in any way a subculture, but this new group brought with it an underground ethos." This is when [Burning Man] began to be imagined as what Hakim Bey called an "interzone" – a secret oasis for an underground, a chink in the armor of society, a place where you can get in and get out, like some artistic Viet Cong, and get away with things. Bey called this "poetic terrorism."

Those early years in the desert were free-wheeling. Anything went. Guns were common. Shooting at stuff from moving cars was a big thing. Burning Man wasn't so much of a city as a vast encampment in the middle of nowhere. The idea was to make the event tough to find, and to take pride in surviving in the hostile environment. Larry Harvey recalls:

> Our settlement began to leapfrog outward, forming a dispersed archipelago of separate campsites – a sort of gold rush in pursuit of individual autonomy. This may have seemed romantic, but it meant that drivers would come rolling into this indecipherable scatter at reckless speeds, particularly at night, and this became a public safety concern.

> In many ways, this secret pirate "interzone" had run amok. Just as we had hidden our city away in the depths of the desert, we

had also hidden our gate. It was, in fact, a gate without a fence; sort of a conceptual gate, like an art installation. If you were lucky enough to find it, you would be instructed to drive so many miles north, and then turn east and drive five or six miles more.[5]

While these Dadaist radicals were dedicated to freedom and self-expression, the early Burning Man culture was not especially interested in an ordered liberty, a new sort of civil society or ecological sustainability.

Burning Man's Critical Transition

In the end, anarchy didn't work out too well.

Sometime after midnight on August 26, 1996, a speeding vehicle ran over two unmarked tents, critically injuring its occupants. At the center of Burning Man, where the theme that year was "inferno," some participants apparently took that theme as a license to play with fire without limits. People used flamethrowers in the open desert. They built multistory wooden structures made to be burned, practically immolating their creators when ignited.

This incident brought into sharp relief a question that had been reverberating among the founders: What was the purpose of Burning Man? And what was the moral intention they wanted to bring to this experiment in the desert? This conflict is captured dramatically in the documentary *Spark: A Burning Man Story* when Larry Harvey says, "It became apparent we were responsible for everybody's welfare. It was on us. We were de facto the state. Which was a conundrum for the hipsters. What does an anarchist say to that?"

On the other side of the argument was the faction of anarchists and Cacophonists who came to the Nevada desert seeking a form of absolute freedom with no bureaucracy, no vehicle restrictions, no rules about guns, and no well-defined perimeter. That position is articulated by exasperated cofounder John Law, who complained: "I didn't want to be a cop! I could see where this was going, we'd need a bureaucratic infrastructure and we'd need to spin stuff. I couldn't do that, I couldn't be part of that."[6]

It brought to the fore the question, What is the relationship between law and freedom? Does law curtail human freedom as Hobbes claimed? Or does law protect and enhance our freedom as Locke argues? Furthermore, who has the authority to make and enforce the law in a free society?"[7]

For Harvey it came down to: Should the event be a civilized affair or a repudiation of order and authority? "If it's a repudiation of order and authority," he said, "and you are the organizer and invite thousands of people, what does that say about you? What kind of a moral position is that?"

The absolutist position of the anarchists might work in small homogeneous groups. But as Burning Man grew it faced the decision all political orders face: What kind of society are we making? How do we trade liberty and security? Harvey worried that cars in the night and the rest of the no-rules world were becoming something of a Hobbsean nightmare: "Things were disconnected and radical and a bit brutal, and you couldn't rely on people for community because there was none. And in the morning there was a political decision to be made: Were we a post-apocalyptic Mad Max society or were we a civil society?"

"For those of us who marched out into the Black Rock Desert in 1990," said Harvey, "there was an underlying irony awaiting us. You see, because there was no context in the desert apart from the context we created, we actually became the Establishment, as organizers of an event. Slowly, step-by-step, circumstances drove us to invent a government. Without intending to, we'd stumbled onto the principle of Civic Responsibility. And maybe this is the essential genius of Burning Man. Out of nothing, we created everything."

For the founders of Burning Man, this was something of Federalist moment – a philosophical turning point in the evolution of this unique interzone. The founders of the United States had wrestled with the same issues – centralized authority versus distributed liberty, and how those structures would enhance or diminish equality. Now those same issues were being worked out on the *playa*.

In short order, Burning Man went from a random place in the desert to a pop-up city designed for self-expression and inclusiveness, a place where roads were marked and public spaces were created for art and communities to flourish. As Harvey recalled:

> As a result of the reforms we put into place in 1997, our city grew more civilized. Instead of driving cars at 100 miles-per-hour with the lights turned off, as was the fashion, people began to encounter one another. Once we eliminated firearms, invented the Greeters, repurposed and reorganized the Rangers, created a street grid, regulated traffic, increased population densities, and gave everyone an address, people could more freely interact. Theme camps tripled, villages thrived, entire neighborhoods began to come alive.

> Perhaps that is the final irony—We ended up creating a world defined by free association and communal aid, rather like that dream of social harmony envisioned by the original anarchists. This was the beginning of the modern phase of Burning Man. The nascent institutions we'd invented, sometimes half in jest, became realities. Our city, many of us felt, had acquired a soul.

The Design of a Civilized City

The self-governing phenomena that plays out at Burning Man today draws on three arenas: 1) The principles and values established by the founders; 2) The emergent activity of thousands of participants, theme camps, and art project teams that embrace these principles as a framework – and then let loose with one of the most imaginative places on earth; and 3) The design of Black Rock City itself. Getting the city right is what sets the stage for the creative explosion that is Burning Man. The city, like all great cities, is a platform for participation and creativity. In a very real sense Black Rock City knows what Jane Jacobs knew: if you get the streets right, if you get the cacophony of street life right, and if a you get scale right you will have a remarkable and flourishing society.

Following the events of 1996, Burning Man undertook a new city design, turning to landscape designer Rod Garrett for a plan. He made a list of 200 urban planning goals looking at how his design might satisfy the greatest number. The design that evolved was a c-shaped semi-circle --- with the giant Man at the center. Several defining elements took shape:

- The inner ring would be deemed the Esplanade, the main street, the boundary between the city and open space home to acres of art projects and roaming art cars, 'mutant vehicles' in the parlance of Burning Man. Camps would form in the residential zones of the outer ring, and the desert in the center would serve as stage for massive art.
- Ordinary cars were banned. Walking, and bicycling became the modes of transportation at Burning Man, with art cars (licensed by the Department of Mutant Vehicles) also serving as the closest thing to public transportation.
- One-third of the city-circle would remain open, connecting the city to the desert and a sense of transcendence. A closed circle might create a sense of constraint and oppressive density. Garrett writes, "We will never further close that arc, as it is humbling to have the vast desert and sky intrude into our self-styled small world. The open side to the circular scheme takes on spiritual and psychological importance. Instead of completely circling the wagons, we invite the natural world to intrude, to lure participants away from our settlement and into the great silence and open space."

You see these principles applied successfully in some of America's best urban experiments. The designers of Boulder, Colorado's pedestrian mall told me that the project works because the mountains in the distance work as a "form of terminus – a place where the city fades into a different environment; the mountains anchor the project as the sea does for Santa Monica's pedestrian mall."[8]

Each design decision helped define the culture. At one point Harvey was asked whether the Black Rock Rangers (volunteers who rescue castaways and provide non-confrontational mediation when needed) ought to have a compound at the center of the city. Instead the center is home to art and civic rituals like the Lamplighters, a nightly procession that places 1,000 lanterns across the city center. Burning Man was to be an art state, not a police state.

These physical cues create a scaffolding for creativity. Your relationship to space changes when you take ownership for authoring it and don't just go to a place that the government or Disneyland makes for you. Radical self-expression and costumes usher you into experimenting with things you might not normally do – further fostering creative play and innovation.

Just as important is a sense of order that's dependable. The concentric circles of streets intersected by radial avenues create a familiar landscape where its almost impossible to get lost. Streets are named alphabetically, and avenues are laid out along the dial of a clock with the civic center (Center Camp) at noon. No matter your state of mind or the hour, if you remember you're camped at 9:30 and B, you can get home.

In 2010, shortly before his death, Garrett wrote about how this design emerged in response to the less friendly prior city:

The new plan was to be strongly affected by our experience of the previous year and the example of 1996, with its disastrous consequence of uncontrolled sprawl. Our goal was to express and abet a sense of communal belonging, and establish population densities that would lead to social interactions. Concurrently, we were attempting to recreate some of the intimacy of our original camping circle, but on a much larger civic scale. Above all, this city needed to work. It was vital that the flow of people and supplies in, out and within were unimpeded. The layout needed to provide for basic services, and be easily comprehended and negotiated. For continuity, it should incorporate familiar features of the previous event sites, and be scalable for future expansion. It also had to facilitate the art and expression of the community, and support past traditions and the principles of Burning Man.

The designer Yves Béhar who started attending Burning Man in 2006 told the *New York Times* that Rod Garrett was a genius in creating a city that was practical, expressive and a source of inspiration, calling it "a circular temporary city plan built around the spectacle of art, music and dance: I wish all cities had such a spirit of utopia by being built around human interaction, community and participation."[9]

These ideas about urban design and life have come to infect Burners and then the real world. Tony Hsieh, a frequent Burner and founder of Zappos, the shoe company, decided to pursue a massive $350 million revitalization of downtown Las Vegas. He's using festival-inspired design and programming to engage people—and to speed up the development of a vibrant city. Container parks and art cars create liveliness and engagement where there was empty space before.

The Las Vegas Downtown Project has collaborated with Burning Man to bring fire-breathing sculptures and art cars to town; several are already delighting residents and attracting families. Hsieh subscribes to Geoffrey West's and Ed Glazer's theories on "urban collisions" – that by putting people in close quarters, creativity happens. That's one reason that Downtown Vegas is all about co-working; the goal is to get people out of the office and into coffee shops and co-working spaces so that connections might happen.

The goal is not to build a smart city but rather "a city that makes you smart," with a TED-style theater so ideas flow every night. Hsieh's team funds startups and then make sure the place is running over with visiting mentors weekly: fashion one week, food the next, tech the next, social entrepreneurs the next, every month. The point is to make the place, like Burning Man, a canvas for hundreds of experiments and reduce the friction to get things started. For example, if you want to start a retail shop, the "container park" can provide cheap short-term leases so one can prototype a pop-up store and if it works, expand it to a permanent one. Try pulling that off in San Francisco.

Art and Culture at Burning Man

"Culture is a wonderful thing to order society," Larry Harvey told *Time* magazine in 2009. "I've noticed that whenever things get tough, the city fathers bring the artists to downtown!"[10] That has certainly been the case in Black Rock City, where art plays a leading role. Each year there are over 350 art installations, not including theme camps and hundreds of wild Mutant Vehicles.

All that art accomplishes more than we might normally expect from "art." At Burning Man, the arts help forge community. They generate focal points around which teams and projects self-organize. Art projects are a principal way that Burning Man spreads its culture of permission, self-expression and agency. The art cars, sculptures, installations and other works are used to tell large-scale, immersive stories. They are a way to get 68,000 people to contemplate major social themes in a collective, almost dream-like manner. In this sense, art at Burning Man helps participants reframe their understanding of the world.

Says Harvey, "I think that art should imitate life. But I'm not happy until life starts to imitate art. Every year we try to create an overarching theme that's about the world. What good is all this if it's not about how to live the rest of your life?"

In a place as tough and unforgiving as the Black Rock Desert, it takes stubborn commitment to get things done. Say you're building a giant steel or wood structure. First there is the challenge of getting the raw materials, along with the required construction equipment, to such a remote location. Then everything has to be assembled amidst extreme temperatures and frequent dust storms. And everywhere is *playa* dust: PH 10, its alkalinity is a bit south of oven cleaner. Particle size: three microns, three times smaller than talc. At Burning Man, it's best to build and appreciate art in a particle mask.

One of the most noteworthy and largest art installations each year is The Temple. The award of the temple commission each year is one of the highest honors in the Burning Man art community, and one of the greatest responsibilities. The temple is a place for contemplation and remembering losses, where hundreds of messages and bits of memorabilia commemorating loved ones are left by Burners each year. While the burning of The Man is always a raucous celebration, the temple burn – the last structure to burn each year – is quiet and somber.

Jess Hobbs, co-founder of Flux Foundation, an Oakland-based collaborative, led The Temple of Flux team in 2012. It was the largest temple yet at Burning Man. Three hundred people spent four months building the abstract wooden structure, which consisted of five double-curved walls that created caves and canyon-like spaces. The piece was approximately one hundred feet deep, two hundred feet wide and forty feet tall. Hobbs told me that while building the temple takes skill and experience, they also invited anyone wishing to participate in the construction to do so. "We call ourselves vision holders. We hold on to the vision. We're not dictating how people get there, we let people choose their roles. You have to remind yourself the whole time this is not your project – 'I am not the owner, I am building a gift that will never be mine, it will be a destination for 60,000 people… And then it will burn!'"

Hobbs' philosophy exemplifies how art actualizes Burning Man's values and inspires the creation of its self-forming city: "Art is a platform for permission. We've grown up in a culture where you hear, 'No' –'No, you don't have the degree for that.' 'No, we don't think you can do that.' 'No, this might not be the place for you.' The overwhelming philosophy at Flux, and the overwhelming philosophy at Burning Man," said Hobbs, "is to say 'Yes.'"[11]

In 2007, Burning Man's art theme was "Green Man," exploring "humanity's relationship to nature." Artist Karen Cusolito and Dan Das Mann created "Crude Awakening," one of the largest works of art ever at Burning Man and still its largest explosion. At the center was a 90 - foot tower styled after its namesake, the Reverend Oil Derrick. Surrounding that were nine steel sculptures of humans from cultures around the world, many thirty feet tall, all worshiping at the altar of fossil fuel, evidently disciples of the flame-throwing religion of unsustainability.

On Saturday night, the Crude Awakening team set off a massive audio-pyrotechnic finale. I was on the *playa* that year, and word spread that this would be the grandest explosion ever at Burning Man – 2,000 gallons of propane and 900 gallons of jet fuel, expertly crafted to combust in a mushroom cloud – the closest thing to an atomic explosion any of us would ever (we hope) witness. I rode my bike about a thousand yards upwind of the tower, contemplating those other Nevada test shots and having no way to gauge what was about to happen. If there was a miscalculation, this might be an excellent place for distant contemplation.

Ritual and Culture

Art here is doing exactly what art is supposed to do: Ask questions, dwell in ambiguity, look at things differently. But because this is Burning Man, it can happen at a scale that is almost impossible anywhere else.

Art and ritual help Burning Man function as a classic liminal experience – a place to get unstuck, to take a new identity and to upend preconceived notions, so that you might come back anew. British anthropologist Victor Turner, author of *From Ritual to Theater: The Human Seriousness of Play*, studied liminality in "primitive" societies, but he could have been writing about Black Rock City. Liminal experiences are ways in which people challenge familiar understandings about their society – where normal limits to thought, self-understanding and behavior are undone and where the very structure of society is "temporarily suspended. These new symbols and constructions then feed back into the 'central' economic incentives, structural models, and *raisons d'etre* of a civilization."[12]

Going up to the desert and getting liminal is useful when change is afoot in society. It's a way to suspend the traditional way of doing things, and, as if in a dream state, imagine and rehearse how things might evolve socially, economically and spiritually.

Turner asserts the whole point of such rituals is to recombine culture into "any and every possible pattern, however weird." If we limit the possible combination of factors to "conventional patterns, designs, or figurations," then we might miss what is "potentially and in principle a free and experimental region of culture, a region where not only new elements but also new combinatory rules may be introduced far more readily."

John Seely Brown, an authority on tech innovation who formerly led Xerox PARC (Palo Alto Research Center), has a contemporary take on the value of art to help us reframe our world, to "regrind our conceptual lenses." At a panel discussion about Burning Man at the Aspen Institute in 2013, he told me, "Artists are not included in our debate on how we build the economy for the future. They're excluded in our nation's emphasis on innovation, which has been left to the STEM [science, technology, engineering, mathematics] crowd. We're not thinking about designing for emergence. Innovation is about seeing the world differently. Who is better at helping us see the world differently than the artists?"[13]

Burning Man in the World

The Burning Man organization is increasingly focused on how to extend its ideas and values beyond the *playa* and into the world. It has organized 225 regional liaisons as the Burning Man Global Leadership Community. The sense of agency and permission Burners bring to the *playa* is often reflected at home, especially in San Francisco, where we use creative play and experimentation to further civic and artistic aims. The Gray Area Foundation for the Arts (where I serve as co-founder and chairman) created the Urban Prototyping Festival to build urban innovation apps and experimental projects in San Francisco, Singapore and London. This year the San Francisco Planning Commission is making citizen prototyping a formal part of city planning along two miles of Market Street. A group called Freespace started by Burner Mike Zuckerman has persuaded landlords in thirteen countries to "gift" unused space to the community as a temporary place to prototype, teach and launch projects.

Michael Yarne, a Burner, former city official and real-estate developer, got fed up with San Francisco's government and launched UP, a nonprofit to promote neighborhood-based "green benefit districts." These are a form of micro-government that allows communities to vote an assessment and have direct and transparent control over hyperlocal projects like mini-parks, green lighting, energy generation and even shared rainwater cisterns for irrigation. The San Francisco Board of Supervisors approved enabling legislation for the program, and Yarne is now looking to take the concept to other cities.

The most visible Burner influence on San Francisco is surely the Bay Lights, arguably the largest public artwork in America. Burner Ben Davis had the idea to transform 1.5 miles of the San Francisco Bay Bridge into a sculpture illuminated by 25,000 light-emitting diodes. It was an audacious act to imagine this iconic, 75-year old bridge as a canvas and then to recruit the support of three San Francisco mayors, secure all the necessary permissions, and raise over seven million dollars in just a couple of years. Artist Leo Villareal, also a Burner, designed the project. He began working with light on the *playa* in 1994 to help find his way back to camp in the vast darkness of the desert night. Today he is one of the top light sculptors in the world, his work now part of the permanent collections of the Museum of Modern Art in New York and the Naoshima Contemporary Art Museum in Kagawa, Japan.

Something all of these projects have in common: each is an Autonomous Zone as imagined by Hakim Bey, whose influence, mediated by Burning Man, has become part of our culture.

Burners Without Borders

Burning Man's most global initiative is Burners Without Borders, a disaster relief and capacity-building nonprofit that draws on the festival's unique ethos and skill set. After Hurricane Katrina struck the Gulf Coast on the very first day of Burning Man in 2005, Brian Behlendorf, founder of Apache Software, recalled the surreal mood on the *playa* when people learned of the devastation and civil breakdown. A food drive and donation effort were immediately organized while groups of Burners began to self-organize treks to the Gulf Coast with heavy equipment and generators in tow.

Upon arriving in Louisiana, Burners set up their headquarters in the parking lot and built what would soon become a distribution center for Oxfam, the Red Cross and other charities. Eventually, the parking lot became a free grocery store for the community. When word got out about what Burners Without Borders was doing, one manufacturer of industrial equipment donated a brand-new heavy loader to the group. Armed with this, Burners Without Borders were completing projects that had once taken days in a matter of hours.

With so much experience in self-organizing their own municipal infrastructure in a hostile environment, Burners are particularly skilled at functioning during chaotic crises when normal services – running water, electricity, communications channels and sanitation systems – are not available. Burners don't just survive in such an environment; they create culture, art, and community there.

BWB founder Carmen Muak told me they learned a lot about how to provide disaster relief in a sustainable manner: "You don't need trailers when you can use domes. You use local materials. You find a way to help the community through its grief." In rural Pearlington, Missisippi, they did just that, both tearing down destroyed structures and building new houses. And then they drew on their Burning Man temple experience. "There was so much beautiful debris around. People had antiques in their homes forever, handed down for generations. You'd find a huge claw-foot dining room table leg, waterlogged chairs. On Saturdays we'd make art together. At night we'd all come together silently for a Burn. It was cathartic."[14] Larry Harvey told me, "FEMA [the Federal Emergency Management Agency] would send in grief councilors. We'd create a temple burn. We found our culture had a lot to offer down there."[15]

Prototype City, Prototype Future

Burning Man the festival is really Burning Man the prototype maker city. It is a place where participants create their urban experience, infrastructure and art. Over its twenty-eight years Burning Man has evolved a balance between top-down structures and curation and a fiercely autonomous, independent community that builds the city as it sees fit. Everyone can be a Robert Moses autonomously green-lighting fanciful projects or a Jane Jacobs using art and culture to forge social capital. It works because the shared community principles work.

Burners also share a similar fear: What if this year is the last? What if this year it gets too big or loses its magic? What if it all goes bland? This sense of paranoia, that the whole thing really might be just a temporary gift, inspires a constant sense of renewal and reinvention. Two years ago my camp, Disorient, decided it was too big and downsized to recapture its culture. It was painful but it worked. When is the last time you heard of a bureaucracy voluntarily dismantling itself to build anew? Ephemeral cites have the advantage of less inertia.

Burning Man fosters great agency and responsibility – a more engaged form of citizenship not just in Black Rock City, but in the real world to which participants return. This ethic is nourished because Black Rock City embraces the prototypical and temporary – which allows for play, learning and immediacy. These are lessons that are being applied to cities around the world through projects such as Freespace, Urban Prototyping, the Bay Lights, the Downtown Porject in Las Vegas, and many other Burner-inspired projects.

Burning Man is also a place to reassess and try out *values* that may have trouble being expressed in our very commercial society. The gifting economy and decommodifcation of experience seem fantastic and redolent of a bygone hippie culture – until we realize that our modern lifestyles are based on unsustainable forms of consumption and that capitalism itself must be reinvented. Burning Man nurtures social capital to consider such challenges.

And yet Burning Man is in the end just a temporary, one-week-a-year city. It is more of a concept car than street-legal vehicle. But like a concept car, it's a collection of new ideas and odd ones ready to be adapted and applied to our world. Burning Man didn't invent the festival, the art car or the Temporary Autonomous Zone any more than Apple invented the personal computer. But like that other venturesome innovator in California, Burning Man executed the concept beautifully, and through its work is having an outsized impact on our culture – and quite possibly on our future.

Peter Hirshberg is chairman of Re:imagine Group, where he shapes strategies at the confluence of people, places, brands and cities. As advisor to United Nations Global Pulse, he has addressed the General Assembly on real-time data for international development. A cofounder of San Francisco's Gray Area Center for Arts and Technology, he has led urban prototyping and open data projects for cities worldwide. Peter was an executive at Apple Computer for nine years, CEO of Elemental Software and Chairman of social media search engine Technorati. He is a senior fellow at the USC Annenberg Center on Communication Leadership and a Henry Crown Fellow of the Aspen Institute.

Notes

[1] Burners take pride in leaving no trace behind and know not to bring in feathers, sequins or any other "moopy-poopy" materials. See http://blog.burningman.com/2012/09/environment/moop-map-live-2012-the-day-we-fail-to-leave-no-trace.

[2] *Time* magazine video, "5 Things Cities Can Learn from Burning Man," [2009], available at http://content.time.com/time/video/player/0,32068,39616455001_1921966,00.html.

[3] Hakin Bay [Peter Lamborn Wilson], *Temporary Autonomous Zones* (Autonomedia, 1991). See also https://en.wikipedia.org/wiki/Temporary_autonomous_zone.

[4] Boyd, Andrew, Mitchell, Dave Oswald, *Beautiful Trouble: A Toolbox for Revolution* (OR Books, 2012).

[5] https://blog.burningman.com/2013/11/tenprinciples/how-the-west-was-won-anarchy-vs-civic-responsibility.

[6] Interview in film, *Spark: A Burning Man Story* (Spark Pictures, 2013); see http://www.sparkpictures.com.

[7] From a dinner conversation between the author and Larry Harvey in London. Referring to the debate about "freedom" that arose after the 1996 events, he told me: "In the end Burning Man is about what is freedom. Nobody lost freedom when we put in rules to keep people from getting run over in the desert." We were discussing the fact that Hobbesean freedom is absolute whereas Lockean freedom (as outlined in his Second Treatise on Civil Government) says, "But though this be a state of *liberty*, yet it is *not* a state of *license*."

[8] Conversation with Daniel Aizenman, LEED AP at the architectural design firm Stantec ViBE, which created the Boulder shopping mall. Aizenman and I were discussing what makes spaces like these work or fail.

[9] Fred A. Bernstein, "Rod Garrett, the Urban Planner Behind 'Burning Man': Its Leadership Lessons, Its Changing Face," *The New York Times*, August 28, 2011, available at http://www.nytimes.com/2011/08/29/arts/rod-garrett-the-urban-planner-behind-burning-man.html.

[10] Larry Harvey quoted in *Time* magazine mini-documentary on Burning Man, 2009. Interview available at https://www.youtube.com/watch?v=EWzohQ1IwB0, see 5:40.

[11] Private conversation with the author. See also Hobbs' talk at the Catalyst Creative series in Downtown Las Vegas on March 27, 2014, an event coproduced by the Downtown Project and Burning Man. See also a talk by Karen Cusolito of American Steel.

[12] Turner, Victor, "Liminal to Liminoid in Play, Flow, and Ritual: An Essay in Comparative Symbology," *Rice University Studies*, 60(3) (1974), pp. 53-92.

[13] Quoted in John Seely Brown's blog, February 2014, at http://www.johnseely-brown.com/newsletter_feb14.html.

[14] Author interview with Carmen Muak, Las Vegas, 2014.

[15] Discussion with Larry Harvey, London, February 2014.

Part II

DIGITAL CURRENCIES AS INSTRUMENTS
FOR SOCIAL CHANGE

Chapter 6

The Internet of Money

By Irving Wladawsky-Berger

IN 2010, THE BBC AND THE British Museum collaborated in a project called "A History of the World." The project sought to tell the history of humanity over the past two million years by examining one hundred objects from the collection of the British Museum.[1] One of the themes was money, which was represented by four objects: one of the world's first gold coins produced in Western Turkey over 2500 years ago; one of the first paper banknotes, a 1375 bill from the Ming Dynasty; a "pieces of eight" silver coin from the late 16th Century, used throughout the Spanish Empire as one of the first global currencies; and a credit card exemplifying the increasingly intangible character of money in the modern world.

Money was not necessary when people lived in small communities where they knew and trusted their neighbors and could therefore exchange labor, food or goods in kind. But the need for something like money arose once communities started to expand and people were dealing with strangers they may never see again and could not trust. It has since played a central role in the rise of civilizations and in human affairs of all kinds. Financial innovations have given rise to commerce and economies, enabled the organization of companies and public institutions, and helped communities become more productive and raise their standard of living.

Money is now undergoing another massive transformation – one that may presage the same order of civilizational change as previous eras experienced. The same digital technologies that are transforming most aspects of our lives are now ushering forth the concept of digital money. This historical transition is going to be one of the most exciting and important societal challenges of the coming decades. Its impact will rival other major technology-based societal transformations, including electricity, radio and TV, and the Internet and World Wide Web.

The evolution to a global digital money ecosystem involves a lot more than the transformation of money (cash, checks, credit and debit cards, etc.) from physical objects in our wallets to digital objects that can now be carried in our smart mobile devices. The coming shift encompasses the whole money ecosystem: the payment infrastructures in use around the world; the financial flows among institutions and between institutions and individuals; government regulatory regimes; the systems for managing personal identities and financial data; the systems for managing security and privacy; and so on. Just about every aspect of the world's economy is involved.

The explosive growth of Internet-connected mobile devices is the driving force behind what we might call the emerging *Internet of Money*. For the past twenty years, the Internet has been an incredible platform for innovation. In its earlier days, the Internet was truly empowering only for those with the means to use it. But ongoing advances in digital technologies are now benefiting just about everyone on the planet. Mobile phones and Internet access have gone from a luxury to a necessity that most everyone can now afford.

A recent McKinsey & Co. study examined the top twelve disruptive technology advances that will transform life, business and the global economy in the coming years.[2] The mobile Internet was at the top of its list:

> Equipped with Internet-enabled mobile computing devices and apps for almost any task, people increasingly go about their daily routines using new ways to understand, perceive and interact with the world. . . However, the full potential of the mobile Internet is yet to be realized; over the coming decade, this technology could fuel significant transformation and disruption, not least from its potential to bring two billion to three billion more people into the connected world, mostly from developing economies.

It's not surprising that advances in information technologies go hand-in-hand with the growing importance of digital money. Money and information have been closely intertwined from time immemorial. Archaeologists and historians have shown that transactional records are among the earliest examples of writing, long predating the minting of gold and silver coins. The oldest known writing system is assumed to have been developed in ancient Mesopotamia around the 4th millennium BC to keep track of information about economic transactions.

It's noteworthy that as physical money is being increasingly replaced by its digital representations somewhere out there in the cloud, we seem to be returning to its ancient roots, where keeping track of money was all about managing information. Not only is money increasingly represented by information, but information about money is itself becoming a form of money. Walter Wriston, chairman and CEO of Citibank from 1967 to 1984 – widely regarded as one of the most influential bankers of his generation – famously said: *"Information about money has become almost as important as money itself."*[3] I think we can now update his remark to read: *"Information about money is money."* Such information is increasingly valuable for personalized marketing, fraud detection and other applications.

Similarly, a recent report by the World Economic Forum, "Personal Data: The Emergence of a New Asset Class," observed: "As some put it, personal data will be the new *oil* – a valuable resource of the 21st century. It will emerge as a new asset class touching all aspects of society."[4] Much of that valuable personal data is related to our past, present and future financial transactions.

In addition, money is inexorably linked to identity and trust. Thus, the transition to universal digital money has to be accompanied by a similar transition to universal digital identity management and to digital trust frameworks. (See Chapter 13, "The ID3 Open Mustard Seed Platform," by Thomas Hardjono et al.) To be effective, digital money must be accompanied by innovations to help us securely identify individuals as they conduct transactions through their mobile devices.

Throughout the world, many poor people cannot prove who they are. Their lack of a birth certificate or some other identity documents excludes them from participating in many of the activities that we take for granted in a modern economy. The Indian government has embarked on a massive Unique ID (UID) initiative known as Aadhaar that aims to issue each resident in India a unique, twelve-digit number.[5] The numbers will be stored in a centralized database and be linked to basic demographics and biometric information.

Among other benefits, Aadhaar will help poor and underprivileged residents of India participate in the world's digital economy, and thus to avail themselves of the many services provided by the government and the private sector. Given the considerable benefits that accrue to everyone – individuals, governments and business – we can expect similar digital identity projects to emerge in economies around the world, but especially in nations where a significant portion of residents have few if any dealings with financial institutions.

The emergence of the *Internet of Money* and new kinds of digital currencies is raising many thorny questions, however: Can digital money ecosystems be based on existing national currencies or do they require entirely new sorts of digital currencies? What about the future of Bitcoin, the most prominent such digital currency?

So far, the development of digital money ecosystems has been almost exclusively based on traditional currencies that all the parties involved understand – e.g., $, £, €, ¥. Most people are reluctant to introduce new digital currencies into the mix, at least at this time, because of the formidable complexities. However, digital currencies, and decentralized cryptocurrencies like Bitcoin in particular, cannot be ignored because they represent significant advances in the development of an Internet-based digital money ecosystem.

The Future of Bitcoin

Bitcoin is both a digital currency and a peer-to-peer payment system. Introduced in 2009, it uses cryptography to control the creation and transfer of money. It's not backed by central governments or banks. The private Bitcoin Foundation manages its technical standards, security concerns and general promotion. As a currency based on open source software, Bitcoin's sophisticated protocols are widely available, which has helped boost its usage and prominence.

The rapid growth of Bitcoin has attracted much attention in recent months, not just because of legal issues (the arrest of an alleged black market trader who used Bitcoin; the bankruptcy of a Bitcoin currency exchange) but because of the actual or perceived threats that Bitcoin and digital currencies pose to the status quo.

One of the most prominent recent commentaries on Bitcoin was "Why Bitcoin Matters," published in the *New York Times* by Marc Andreessen, the technologist, entrepreneur and investor.[6] Andreessen compares Bitcoin in 2014 to personal computers in 1975 and the Internet in 1993: an embryonic technology poised to take off. His VC firm, Andreessen Horowitz, has invested close to $50 million in Bitcoin-related start-ups and continues to actively search for additional such investment opportunities. In his column, Andreessen pointed out that there is an enormous gulf between what the press, economists and others believe Bitcoin is, and what a number of technologists and entrepreneurs like him are so excited about:

> First, Bitcoin at its most fundamental level is a breakthrough in computer science – one that builds on 20 years of research into cryptographic currency, and 40 years of research in cryptography, by thousands of researchers around the world. . . Bitcoin gives us, for the first time, a way for one Internet user to transfer a unique piece of digital property [e.g., money, signatures, contracts, stocks and bonds] to another Internet user, such that the transfer is guaranteed to be safe and secure, everyone knows that the transfer has taken place, and nobody can challenge the legitimacy of the transfer. The consequences of this breakthrough are hard to overstate.

Andreessen lauds Bitcoin as a new kind of peer-to-peer payment system – "a way to exchange money or assets between parties with no preexisting trust. . . the first Internet-wide payment system where transactions either happen with no fees or very low fees (down to fractions of pennies). Existing payment systems charge fees of about

2 to 3 percent – and that's in the developed world. In lots of other places, there either are no modern payment systems or the rates are significantly higher."

As a digital currency, Bitcoin has been quite volatile, with large fluctuations in value over days, weeks and months. In early 2014, the exchange rate of a bitcoin was fluctuating between $500 and $900. Its volatility is largely due to speculation and relatively low payment volumes. Despite its positive qualities as a highly secure digital payment system, many believe that the currency's volatility will likely drive away the vast majority of individuals and merchants. Andreessen disagrees:

> The criticism that merchants will not accept Bitcoin because of its volatility is also incorrect. Bitcoin can be used entirely as a payment system; merchants do not need to hold any Bitcoin currency or be exposed to Bitcoin volatility at any time. Any consumer or merchant can trade in and out of Bitcoin and other currencies any time they want.

A few weeks ago, technology journalist Glenn Fleishman wrote an article refuting a number of Andreessen's arguments.[7] The article starts out by agreeing that Bitcoin represents a major innovation in payment systems:

> I agree with Andreessen that Bitcoin is the first practical, large-scale mechanism to deal with the problem of decentralizing trust – no parties need know each other nor trust each other for transactions to complete successfully, verifiably and irrevocably. . . I also agree completely with Andreessen that Bitcoin can be used for an enormous number of non-currency related purposes in which permanent, irreversible proofs of transactions are required.

But he then goes on to argue with many of the points made by Andreessen, including Bitcoin's liquidity and low fees, and its claimed advantages in preventing fraud, theft and other illegal activities. This past November, Fleishman published an article in *The Economist*, "Bitcoin under Pressure," which carried the tag line: "It is mathematically elegant, increasingly popular and highly controversial. Bitcoin's success is putting it under growing strain."[8] He goes on to explain his concerns:

> Bitcoin's success has revealed three weaknesses in particular. It is not as secure and anonymous as it seems; the mining system that both increases the Bitcoin supply and ensures the integrity of the currency has led to an unsustainable computational arms-race; and the distributed-ledger system is becoming unwieldy. Will Bitcoin's self-correcting mechanisms, and the enlightened self-interest of its users, be able to address these weaknesses and keep Bitcoin on the rails? . . . Perhaps Bitcoin, like the Internet, will smoothly evolve from a quirky experiment to a trusted utility. But it could also go the way of Napster, the trailblazing music-sharing system that pioneered a new category, but was superseded by superior implementations that overcame its technical and commercial flaws.

Fleishman believes that Bitcoin offers an opportunity to reimagine how the financial system can and should work in the Internet era. But he makes a distinction between its future as a technology and its future as a currency. "Bitcoin shows a path for massively more secure, reliable and sensible ways to store value and move it around. As a currency, I have little faith that it will become a replacement for dollars, euros or renminbi. As a model for a future payment and transaction system, I believe it's already shown its value."

Fleishman's conclusion, which I agree with, is similar to that of top payments expert Karen Webster, who wrote at the end of 2013: "Our prediction is that those who are in the best position to exploit Bitcoin's success will be those who recognize that there's a difference between the technology that enables Bitcoin and Bitcoin the currency and will invest in perfecting the former and not the latter."[9]

A number of recent articles have been quite negative. At a panel in the 2014 World Economic Forum in Davos, Yale economist and Nobel Laureate Robert Schiller said that Bitcoin "is just an amazing example of a bubble." As reported in *Business Insider*, Schiller said that while he finds Bitcoin to be an inspiration because of the computer science, he does not think of it as an economic advance and views it as a return to the dark ages. Schiller, an expert on economic bubbles, believes that much of its fascination is due to its extreme volatility. [10]

Another Nobel Prize-winning economist, Paul Krugman, chose the title "Bitcoin is Evil" for one of his recent *New York Times* columns.[11] Krugman's main reason for his negative views is similar to that of author Charlie Stross, who wrote a strong critique of Bitcoin called "Why I Want Bitcoin to Die in a Fire." Stross writes:

> Like all currency systems, Bitcoin comes with an implicit political agenda attached. Decisions we take about how to manage money, taxation and the economy have consequences: by its consequences you may judge a finance system. . . Bitcoin looks like it was designed as a weapon intended to damage central banking and money issuing banks, with a Libertarian political agenda in mind – to damage states' ability to collect tax and monitor their citizens financial transactions.[12]

Finally, there is the question whether Bitcoin and other virtual currencies should be subject to financial regulations similar to those currently in place for existing currencies. Anti-money laundering is one such regulation enforced by governments around the world to curtail illicit activities like the flow of money from the drug trade and the financing of terrorist activities. Bitcoin has been linked to such illicit activities, which has led to a few recent arrests.

Governments have started looking at how to regulate Bitcoin and similar digital currencies.

A recent *New York Times* article, "More Bitcoin Regulation is Inevitable," concluded: "The days of anonymous transactions in Bitcoin and operating an exchange with no outside interference are over. As virtual currencies develop, firms devoted to aiding trading, and perhaps even their users, will encounter greater government regulation, along with the costs that come with compliance."[13]

Most everyone agrees that for the foreseeable future, the bulk of the money flowing in digital money ecosystems will continue to be based on existing currencies, with digital currencies playing important niche roles. Given Bitcoin's current problems, it's not clear whether it will be one of the surviving digital currencies. But regardless of Bitcoin's fate, its cryptographic advances, distributed architecture and other key technologies will play major roles in the development of a digital money ecosystem for the Internet era.

Irving Wladawsky-Berger spent 37 years at IBM, where his primary focus was on innovation and technical strategy. He led a number of IBM's companywide initiatives including the Internet and e-business, supercomputing and Linux. In March 2008, Wladawsky-Berger joined Citi as Strategic Advisor, working on innovation and technology initiatives including the transition to mobile digital money and payments. He is Visiting Lecturer at M.I.T., Adjunct Professor at Imperial College, and Executive-in-Residence at NYU's Center for Urban Science and Progress. In April 2012 he became a regular contributor to the Wall Street Journal's CIO Journal.

Notes

[1] BBC, "A History of the World in 100 Objects," at http://www.bbc.co.uk/ahistoryoftheworld.

[2] James Manyika, Michael Chui et al., McKinsey Global Institute, "Disruptive Technologies: Advances that Will Transform Life, Business and the Global Economy," May 2013, at http://www.mckinsey.com/insights/business_technology/disruptive_technologies?cid=disruptive_tech-eml-alt-mip-mck-oth-1305.

[3] World Economy Forum, "Personal Data: The Emergence of a New Asset Class," January 2011, available at http://www3.weforum.org/docs/WEF_ITTC_PersonalDataNewAsset_Report_2011.pdf.

[4] Thomas A. Bass, "The Future of Money," *Wired*, October 1996, at http://www.wired.com/wired/archive/4.10/wriston.html.

[5] "Reform by Numbers," *The Economist*, January 14, 2012, available at http://www.economist.com/node/21542814.

[6] Marc Andreessen, "Why Bitcoin Matters," *The New York Times*, January 21, 2014, available at http://nyti.ms/1cQPoqa.

[7] Glenn Fleishman, "On the Matter of Why Bitcoin Matters," *The Magazine on Medium*, available at https://medium.com/the-magazine/23e551c67a6.

[8] "Bitcoin under Pressure," *The Economist*, November 27, 2013, available at http://www.economist.com/news/technology-quarterly/21590766-virtual-currency-it-mathematically-elegant-increasingly-popular-and-highly.

[9] Karen Webster, "Looking Ahead at the Close of 2013," *Pymnts.com*, available at http://www.pymnts.com/briefing-room/consumer-engagement/Loyalty/2013/looking-ahead-at-the-close-of-2013.

[10] Joe Weisenthal, "Robert Shiller: Bitcoin is an Amazing Example of a Bubble," January 24, 2014, available at http://www.businessinsider.com/robert-shiller-bitcoin-2014-1.

[11] Paul Krugman, "Bitcoin is Evil," *The New York Times*, December 28, 2013, available at http://krugman.blogs.nytimes.com/2013/12/28/bitcoin-is-evil/?_php=true&_type=blogs&_r=0.

[12] Charlie Stross, "Why I Want Bitcoin to Die in a Fire," *Charlie's Diary*, December 28, 2013, available at http://www.antipope.org/charlie/blog-static/2013/12/why-i-want-bitcoin-to-die-in-a.html.

[13] Peter J. Hernning, "More Bitcoin Regulation Is Inevitable," *The New York Times*, February 3, 2014, available at http://dealbook.nytimes.com/2014/02/03/more-bitcoin-regulation-is-inevitable/?_php=true&_type=blogs&_php=true&_type=blogs&ref=business&_r=1.

Chapter 7

Why Complementary Currencies
Are Necessary to Financial Stability:
The Scientific Evidence

By Bernard Lietaer

CONVENTIONAL ECONOMISTS TEND TO REGARD complementary currencies as an anomaly, to be dismissed as an irrelevant or romantic distraction. Regulators tolerate them, as long as they remain marginal. If any were ever to grow to a relevant size, they believe such monetary innovations should be suppressed lest they disturb monetary policy or reduce the efficiency of the price formation process.[1]

But this belief is incorrect: A recent scientific breakthrough provides evidence that a monopoly of one single type of currency is a systemic cause for the prevailing monetary and financial instability. In fact, it will be shown that, far from being a disturbance, a variety of monetary media is necessary for economic and financial stability in a society. This conclusion stems from a structural flaw in our modern monetary system, a flaw that has played an unacknowledged role in every crash since the Dutch tulip bubble burst in 1637, including the one we are experiencing now!

The proof for this claim comes from fundamental laws that govern all *complex flow systems*, including natural ecosystems, economic and financial systems. Recent theoretical breakthroughs now make it possible to measure quantitatively, with a single metric, the sustainability of any complex flow system, based on the emergent properties of its structural diversity and interconnectivity. Furthermore, we can now see that whenever diversity in a complex flow network is being sacrificed because of too much emphasis on efficiency, systemic collapses are a totally predictable consequence.

For generations, we have been living worldwide with a mono-culture of the same type of media of exchange – a single national currency monopoly in each country, created everywhere through bank-issued debt. Neither Marxist nor various capitalist schools of economic thought find this troubling. The main difference in this respect between communism of the Marxist-Leninist variety on the one side, and capitalism on the other, is that in the former, governments always own the banks. While in the latter, governments own the banks only after they have gone bankrupt. Indeed, in capitalism, private investors are normally supposed to be in control.

But the functioning of the money system itself is the same in both instances: both rely on a single national currency created through bank debt. The structural solution to economic and financial instability in both cases is also clear, even if it appears shockingly unorthodox: we need to diversify the types of currencies available in a society and the types of agents that are creating them, specifically through complementary currencies.

The Sustainability of Complex Flow Systems

We now can demonstrate that a structural fault is involved in generating financial crashes. Quantitative ecological research has provided empirical substantiation of this mechanism and a deeper understanding of its dynamics. A fully documented, step-by-step mathematical proof of the claims made below can be found in a seminal paper by Ulanowicz, Goerner, Lietaer and Gomez, whose most relevant points are summarized here.[2]

Information is any "difference that makes the difference," Gregory Bateson famously declared, and, as the binary logic of the digital age has popularized, such difference almost always involves the *absence* of something. Information theory (IT), in studying the working of whole systems, is a means for apprehending and quantifying what is missing from representations. The key point is that if one is to address the issue of sustainability, then the inchoate, undetermined "potentiality" of a system must also become the focus of inquiry, because it is the source of the resilience that allows the entire system to persist.[3]

What IT tells us is that a system's capacity to undergo change has two components: an order component, called "mutual constraint," quantifies all that is regular, orderly, coherent and efficient. It encompasses basically all the concerns of conventional science. This first component is an analogue of Newton's Third Law of Motion, or of the Chinese *Yang* construct.

By contrast, the second component represents the lack of those same attributes, or the irregular, disorderly, incoherent and inefficient potential behaviors that have escaped the scrutiny of science. They are ignored or discounted mainly because they cannot easily be described, are less readily repeated or measured, or all of the above. This component corresponds to the Chinese *Yin*.

In the jargon of IT, this second, usually overlooked component of system change is called "conditional entropy"; it can also be thought of as uncommitted potential. The very absence of order (even if its potential is never activated and therefore goes unnoticed and unmeasured) plays the key role in a system's long-term stability. This uncommitted potential enables a system to adapt to a changing environment and survive unexpected challenges.

If we are to understand sustainability, we must recognize that the absence of order is even more significant than the first variable, order. A living system adapts in homeostatic fashion to buffer variability in performance by expending what Odum called "reserves."[4] The reserve in this case is not some palpable storage such as a cache of some material resource. Rather, it is the capacity to show flexibility and adaptability to new circumstances – and it usually requires some loss of efficient performance.[5] Systems that endure – that is, are sustainable – are able to achieve a dynamic balance between these two poles of order and disorder, efficient performance and adaptive resilience.

Let us now define more precisely our terminology:

- *Efficiency* is defined as the capacity of a complex flow system to process a given volume of whatever flows through it, per unit of time – e.g., grams of biomass per square meter per year for a natural ecosystem; GDP per capita in an economy; or billions of dollars per day in an electronic payment system.

- *Resilience* is the capacity of a complex flow network to survive an attack, a disease, or adapt to a change in its environment.

A crucial finding from the study of complex flow systems is that efficiency is definitely not a sufficient metric for achieving sustainability. Metrics such as GDP or return on investment to capital are not sufficient to assess economic sustainability because they cannot distinguish between healthy sustainable growth and short-term bubbles doomed to collapse. For a complex flow system to be sustainable, it must possesses enough *resilience*, which can be understood as an undefined and contingent responsiveness to the unpredictable challenges thrown up by a system's own workings and its environment.

A Chinese Insight

"When *Yang* and *Yin* combine appropriately, all things achieve harmony," according to Lao Tse in *Tao Te King* #42. This dialectic between efficiency and resilience is the "go and get" and the "let go and give" of life. In the Chinese philosophical tradition, *yang* and *yin* characteristics are assigned to all natural systems. In Asia the concepts of *Yin-Yang* are seen as necessary complements to each other. Their history goes back thousands years, to Siberian shamanism and to the *Yi Jing* (the Book of Changes), attributed to King Wen of Zhou (1099-1050 BC). The explicit *Weltanschauung* of Chinese philosophy is precisely the need for all aspects of nature and life to strike an appropriate balance between *Yang* and *Yin* energies.

For the first time in history, to our knowledge, Western science is now able to prove in a quantitative way the validity and depth of this Taoist discovery. So let us give credit to this ancient Eastern insight that has been so widely ignored in the West, to the point we don't even have words to express this idea.

C.G. Jung was one of the first to express regret that our Western culture is not more familiar with the concept of *Yang* and *Yin*: "Unfortunately, our Western mind, lacking all culture in this respect, has never yet devised a concept, nor even a name, for the 'union of opposites through the middle path', that most fundamental item of inward experience, which could respectably be set against the Chinese concept of Tao." If our use of this *Yin-Yang* vocabulary risks appearing exotic, it is simply because we don't have any equivalent words in any of our Western languages.

Oriental philosophers have developed an infinite number of ways to describe the *Yin-Yang* relationship and polarity. The following figure offers those selected as most relevant for our purpose. The following figure identifies attributes most relevant to our inquiry here.

Yin-Yang Characteristics

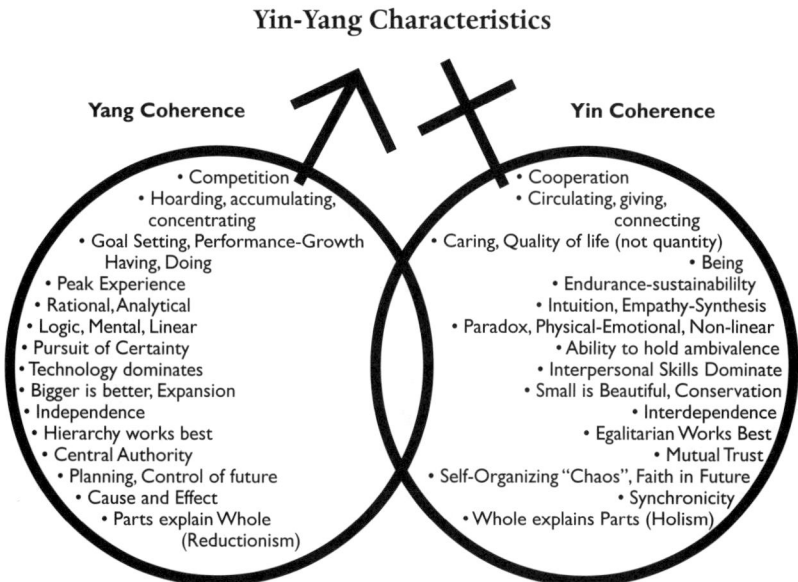

Yang Coherence

- Competition
- Hoarding, accumulating, concentrating
- Goal Setting, Performance-Growth Having, Doing
- Peak Experience
- Rational, Analytical
- Logic, Mental, Linear
- Pursuit of Certainty
- Technology dominates
- Bigger is better, Expansion
- Independence
- Hierarchy works best
- Central Authority
- Planning, Control of future
- Cause and Effect
- Parts explain Whole (Reductionism)

Yin Coherence

- Cooperation
- Circulating, giving, connecting
- Caring, Quality of life (not quantity)
- Being
- Endurance-sustainabililty
- Intuition, Empathy-Synthesis
- Paradox, Physical-Emotional, Non-linear
- Ability to hold ambivalence
- Interpersonal Skills Dominate
- Small is Beautiful, Conservation
- Interdependence
- Egalitarian Works Best
- Mutual Trust
- Self-Organizing "Chaos", Faith in Future
- Synchronicity
- Whole explains Parts (Holism)

Fig. 1: Some Yin-Yang Coherences and Polarities

This figure can be read vertically, emphasizing the internal coherences. Or it can be read horizontally, emphasizing the polarity between them. One advantage in using the *Yin-Yang* vocabulary is that Taoists never separate such polarities. They emphasize the connection between them – their *complementarity* – because, in truth, both are indispensable!

The *Yin* and *Yang* ways of looking at reality are not competing ways of relating to and interpreting reality any more than your right eye "competes" with your left one. Instead, because of their differences, they together provide you with a range and depth of vision, something which neither one can do by itself.

For the past millennia, all patriarchal societies have tended to confer more legitimacy on the male half of human perception. We have thereby projected a hierarchical duality on concepts such as activity/passivity, creativity/receptivity, culture/nature, mind/senses, spirit/matter, invariably claiming the former to be somehow "better" or more "accurate" than the latter. What matters here is not to deny the qualities inherent in the masculine viewpoint, but to elevate the feminine to an equal level. A shift in consciousness towards giving equal emphasis to both views is not just a matter of fairness; it may be the key to developing the kind of integrated, synergistic vision needed for the sustainability of our species.

"The feminine and the masculine are not objects, not things, not simply biological bodies we are attempting to unite," writes Molly Dwyer, "but rather complex, archetypal organizations of consciousness…What is needed is a recognition of the synergy between these polar opposites. Synergy is evident everywhere in nature, and is an important source of causation in the ongoing evolutionary process. Since the relationship between male and female is fundamentally synergistic, it is essential that we rethink and recreate our cultural and symbolic understanding of the feminine and its relationship to the masculine to increase the possibility that the human species will co-create an evolutionary change that is advantageous to the entire biosphere. If we do not, we are in danger of bringing about our own extinction…"[6]

Not surprisingly, in all patriarchal societies a *Yang* bias is accepted as "normal." In contrast, the poet John Keats coined the term "negative capability" for the often overlooked *Yin* trait of human personality and experience: the capacity to hold uncertainty without angst – the capacity to live with the unknown as an ally rather than something to be eliminated. It is more like a connection to an undifferentiated ground that resists form, which continually invokes questions and reflection and is potentially multidimensional, a space of "both-and" and *neti-neti*, the Hindu concept literally meaning "neither this, nor that."

In summary, natural ecosystems exist because they have both sufficient self-directed identity and flexibility to change. The polarities necessitate each other in an appropriate balance of harmonious complementarity. Over time, nature must have solved many of the structural problems in ecosystems. Otherwise, these ecosystems simply wouldn't exist today. They are our best living examples of large-scale and long-term sustainability in action.

Empirical Ecological Evidence

A key insight from empirical studies of natural systems is that nature does not select for maximum efficiency, but for a balance between the two opposing poles of efficiency and resilience. Because both are indispensable for long-term sustainability and health, the healthiest flow systems are those that are closest to an optimal balance between these two opposing pulls. Conversely, an excess of either attribute leads to systemic instability. Too much efficiency (excess *Yang*) leads to brittleness and too much resilience (excess *Yin*) leads to stagnation. The former is caused by too little diversity and connectivity, and the latter by too much diversity and connectivity. This dynamic is illustrated in Fig. 2.

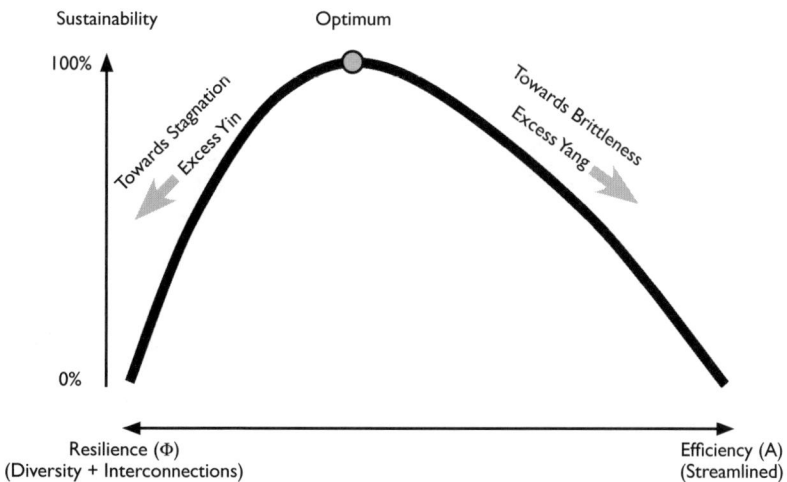

Fig. 2: The effects of diversity and connectivity in achieving efficiency and resilience.

Sustainability of a complex flow system can therefore be defined as *the optimal balance between efficiency and resilience in its network*. With these distinctions we are now able to define and precisely quantify a complex system's sustainability in a single metric.

In human designed systems, there may be a tendency to over-emphasize efficiency and growth of volume at the expense of resilience – that is, to emphasize efficiency more than resilience. Resilience theory suggests that autocatalytic forces can jeopardize the sustainability of the whole network. In an economy, for example, the larger economic actors may use lobbying to obtain laws and rules that favor their growth at the expense of the smaller ones. In the financial domain, banks may become "too big to fail" and thereby obtain implicit government guarantees that they will be bailed out in case of trouble.

In such cases, sustainability is dramatically reduced because interconnectivity collapses. In the monetary domain, similarly, as long as we remain stuck with the idea of a single national currency, the system is structurally configured to reduce diversity. Such a system will predictably collapse, and if it is forcibly restored to "normal," it will collapse again and again. When a bias favoring efficiency is pushed still further, the collapse of interconnectivity and sustainability grows worse, hastening the speed of a system's collapse.

Interestingly, there is an asymmetry in natural systems versus economic systems. In natural ecosystems optimality requires greater resilience than efficiency! In natural ecosystems the weight on efficiency has empirically been determined from a regression analysis using actual data from a wide variety of ecosystems of different scales that the optimal point lies closer to resilience than efficiency.

Moving beyond information theory, ecologists have measured the transfer of biomass and energy ("trophic exchanges") within ecosystems. They have also found ways to derive values for an ecosystem's throughput efficiency and resilience by estimating network size and network connectedness in terms of two structural variables: diversity and interconnectivity. It turns out that there is a specific zone of optimal robustness into which all observed natural ecosystems fall.

This zone has been named the "Window of Viability" (in ecological literature the "Window of Vitality"), as illustrated in Fig. 3.

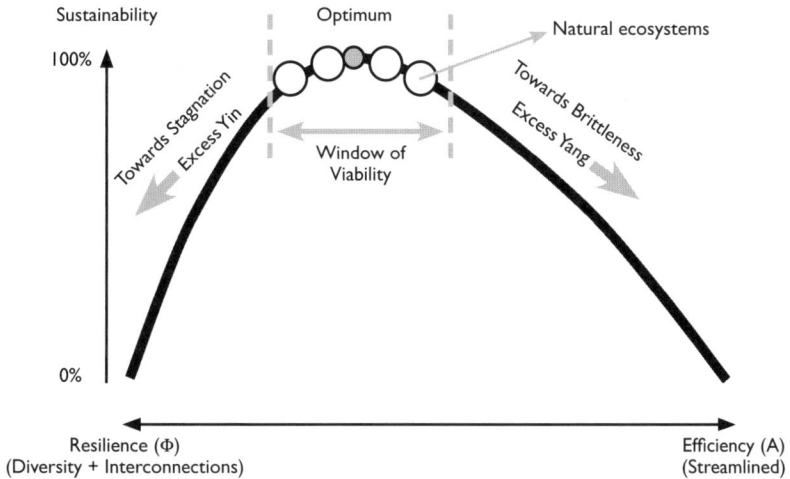

Fig. 3: The Window of Viability

Application to Other Complex Flow Systems

A reasonable question arises: Do the lessons we learn from ecosystems truly apply to other complex flow systems, such as economic or financial systems? It appears to be so. It is critical to understand that the findings described in natural ecosystems arise from the very structure of a complex flow system, and therefore that they remain valid for any complex flow network with a similar structure, regardless of what is being processed in the system. It can be biomass in an ecosystem, information in a biological system, electrons in an electrical power network, or money in an economic system. This is precisely one of the strong points of using a web-like network approach instead of machine-like metaphor.

The fields of engineering, business and economics each focus almost exclusively on efficiency, which means that we have rich opportunities to empirically test whether the proposed metrics for complex flow systems would indeed improve sustainability.

For example, electrical power grids had been systematically optimized for decades towards ever-greater technical and economic efficiency. It has come as a surprise to many engineers that, as they have approached higher efficiencies, suddenly large-scale blackouts have been breaking out with a vengeance "out of nowhere." A few decades ago several blackouts hit large areas of the United States and northern Germany. The data should be available to model these systems as flow networks, because that is what they literally are. One could then quantify their efficiency and resilience, and plot their Window of Viability. The solution on how to rebalance the power grid system to make it less brittle, and to determine its optimal sustainability, would be an obvious "hard science" test application of the concepts and metrics described here.

The point being made here is truly profound and has wide-reaching implications for all complex systems, natural or human-made. Placing too much emphasis on efficiency tends to automatically maximize flows, size and consolidation at the expense of choice, connectivity and resilience until the entire system becomes unstable and collapses. And yet conventional engineering, economics and finance invariably assume that more efficiency is always better!

Until these findings about resilience and the Window of Viability, the only means for identifying the relative success of a system, whether in nature or in economics, have been measures of total throughput and efficiency. For example, in ecosystems, as in economies, size is generally measured as the total volume of system throughput/activity. Gross Domestic Product (GDP) measures the size of economies in this fashion and Total System Throughput (TST) does the same for ecosystems. Many economists urge endless growth in size (GDP) because they assume that growth in size is a "good enough" proxy metric for a system's health.

GDP and TST, however, are both poor measures of sustainable viability because they ignore network structure. They cannot, for example, distinguish between a healthily thriving resilient economy and a bubble that is doomed to burst. Or between healthy "development," as Herman Daly describes it,[7] and explosive growth in monetary exchanges driven by runaway speculation. Now, however, we can distinguish whether a particular increase in throughput and efficiency is a sign of healthy growth or just a relatively short-term bubble that is doomed to collapse.

Application to Financial and Monetary Systems

Applying the above complex flow framework specifically to financial and monetary systems, we can predict that an excessive focus on efficiency will tend to create exactly the kind of bubble economy that we have been able to observe repeatedly in every boom and bust cycle in history, including the biggest bust of them all, the one triggered in 2007-8 whose fallout we are still dealing with today.

If we view economies as flow systems, the primary function of money as a medium of exchange can be seen as critical. Money is to the real economy as biomass is to an ecosystem – an essential vehicle for catalyzing processes, allocating resources, and generally allowing the exchange system to work as a synergetic whole. The connection to structure is immediately apparent. In economies, as in ecosystems and living organisms, the health of the whole depends heavily on the structure by which the catalyzing medium – in this case, money – circulates among businesses and individuals. Money must continue to circulate in sufficiency to all corners of the whole because poor circulation will strangle either the supply side or the demand side of the economy, or both.

Our global monetary system is itself obviously a flow network structure, in which monopolistic national currencies flow within each country (or group of countries in the case of the Euro), and interconnect on a global level. The technical justification for enforcing a monopoly of a single currency within each country is to optimize the efficiency of price formation and exchanges in national markets. Strict regulations in every country maintain these monopolies. Banking institutional regulations further ensure that banks tend to be carbon copies of each other both in terms of their structure and behavior. The consequences of relying on a worldwide monoculture of big banks were demonstrated with the cataclysmic, simultaneous crash of 2008.

In a seminal 1953 paper, Milton Friedman proposed letting markets determine the value of each national currency as a way to further improve the overall efficiency of the global monetary system. [8] This idea was actually implemented by President Nixon in 1971 to avoid a run on the dollar at that time. Since then, an extraordinarily efficient and sophisticated global communications infrastructure has been built to link and trade these national currencies. According to the Bank of International Settlements, the trading volume in the foreign exchange markets reached an impressive $5.3 trillion per day in 2013, to which trillions of currency derivatives should be added. Over 95 percent of that trading volume is speculative, and less than 5 percent is in fact used for actual international trade of goods and services.

Speculation can play a positive role in any market: theory and practice show that it can improve market efficiency by increasing liquidity and depth in the market.* But current speculative levels are clearly out of balance. Although over half a century old, John Maynard Keynes' opinion has never been as appropriate as it is today: "Speculators may do no harm as bubbles on a steady stream of enterprise. But the position is serious when enterprise becomes the bubble on a whirlpool of speculation. When the capital development of a country becomes a byproduct of the activities of a casino, the job is likely to be ill-done."[9]

Nobody questions the efficiency of these huge markets; but their lack of resilience has been vividly demonstrated by the Asian crisis of the late 1990s and dozens of other monetary crashes. Our global network of monopolistic national moneys has evolved into an overly efficient and therefore dangerously brittle system. The system's lack of resilience shows up not in the technical field of the computer networks (which all have backups), but in the financial realm. Such a crisis, particularly a combined monetary and banking crash, is – apart from war – the worst thing that can happen to a country.

---

*   "Liquidity" and "depth" in financial markets refer to the possibility of moving large volumes of money without significantly affecting prices. In a deep market, a lot of people are buying and selling. By contrast, in a thin market, because fewer people are trading, even one single large transaction could significantly affect prices.

Even more ironically, whenever a banking crisis unfolds, governments invariably step in to help the larger banks to absorb the smaller ones, believing that the efficiency of the system is thereby further increased. This makes banks that are "too big to fail" into still bigger ones, until they become "too big to bail."

As noted earlier, the substance that circulates in our global economic network – money – is maintained as a monopoly of a single type of currency: bank-debt money, created with interest. Imagine a planetary ecosystem where only one single type of plant or animal is tolerated and artificially maintained, and where any manifestation of successful diversity is eradicated as an inappropriate "competitor" because it would reduce the efficiency of the whole. It would clearly be unsustainable.

An overly efficient system is "an accident waiting to happen," destined to suffer a sudden crash and collapse however many competent people dedicate time and heroic efforts to try to manage it. After a collapse, in both natural ecosystems and in monetary systems, however, the lessons of resilient systems are not learned. Political and market authorities seek to restore the preexisting structures and the same process resumes again. We have seen this after the complete meltdowns of the financial systems in Germany in the 1920s and again at the end of World War II; in the United States during the "bank holidays" of the Great Depression; in Russia in the 1990s; and in Argentina in 1999-2002. All were simultaneous monetary and banking crises. In our time, a dollar or a Euro crisis could trigger a similar phenomenon.

Fortunately, most crises are less extreme than that. However, going through the exercise of exploring such a "pure" extreme gives some ideas of the power and depth of the dynamics involved. Less extreme crises manifest only some of the features of the process we have described. Just like a partial forest fire, one that doesn't reduce everything to ashes, these scenarios manifest only some of the attributes of a total burnout.

The process of a collapse shows up graphically with a drop of sustainability to close to 0 percent, as shown in Fig. 4. The next step after a total meltdown is an extreme fragmentation, without much collaboration. In a forest, this takes the form of seedlings of any type trying to sprout randomly. At the extreme, in a financial system, this takes the form of a return to primitive barter – i.e., survival exchanges without any standardization or organization. This stage can be seen as the case when each participant uses whatever he or she has as a commodity currency.

The next step is the emergence of a multitude of "survival organizations" that start to introduce some standards and some informal agreements on dates and places where the exchanges may take place. In Argentina this took the form of the multiplication of local exchange mechanisms, under the names of *ruedes de trueque* in which locally issued *creditos* currencies were used as medium of exchange in weekly neighborhood markets. Assuming that the designs of these systems were sound (which unfortunately wasn't the case in Argentina), then the better systems would tend to emerge as models for others, and gradually more efficient exchange systems would evolve. Over time, a more diversified and more interconnected economy would rebuild, which would return the system back into the zone of the Window of Viability. This whole process is illustrated in Fig. 4.

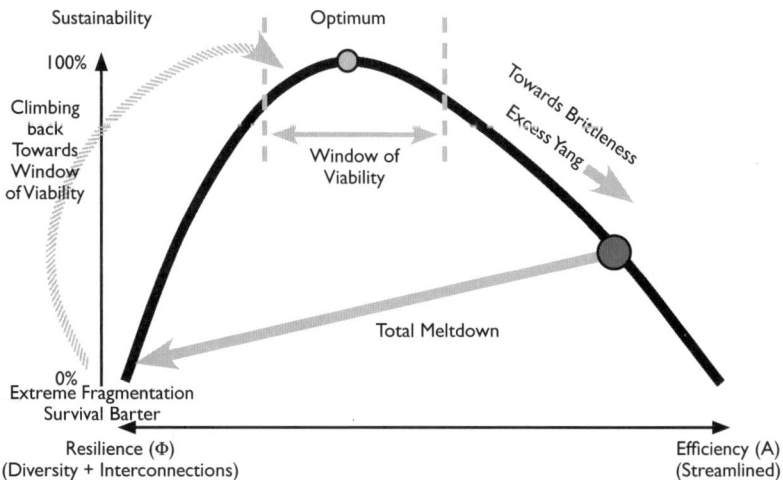

Fig. 4: The Aftermath of a Total Meltdown in a Natural Ecosystem. After extreme fragmentation the species that are best adapted to the new environment slowly make the flow system climb back toward the Window of Viability.

In modern monetary practice, this scenario does not occur, however. What has invariably happened is that – thanks to orthodox monetary policies and bank lobbying – a monopoly of bank debt money is reestablished as the only legitimate medium of exchange. This took place for instance in Germany in the 1920s and in the US in the 1930s, when all the "emergency currencies" were outlawed; or in Argentina through a massive falsification of *creditos* paper currencies (see Fig. 5).

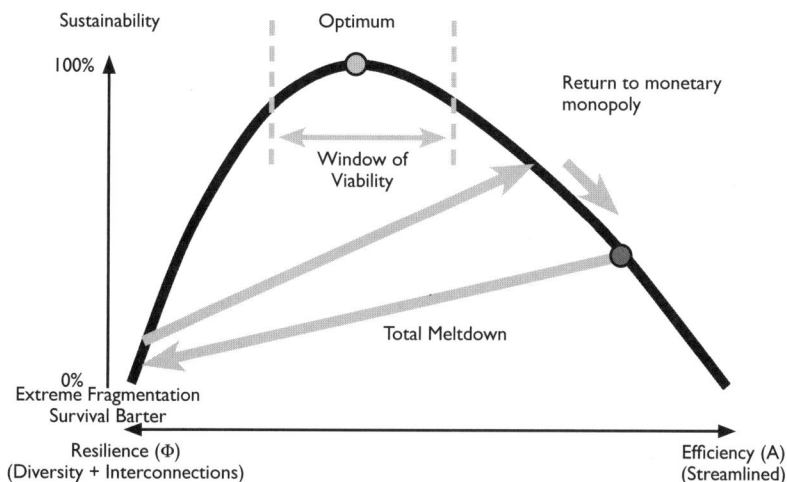

Fig. 5: No Window of Viability in a Monetary Monoculture. *After a monetary or financial collapse, however, a monetary monoculture is reestablished as soon as possible, with the result that the return to a Window of Viability is not allowed to emerge. This guarantees that we continue repeatedly to go through this loop.*

We now know that such a monoculture is not a sustainable structure in the long run. Attempts to return to "normalcy" will in fact overshoot the window of sustainability again. The system will resume the next cycle of boom and bust by pushing for greater efficiency within a monoculture environment, which seeds the next crash later.

We have been going through this loop many times by now. According to International Monetary Fund (IMF) data, since the 1970s there have been no less than 145 banking crises, 208 monetary crashes and 72 sovereign debt crises: a staggering total of 425 systemic crises, an average of more than ten countries per year![10] These crises have hit more than three-quarters of the 180 countries that are members of the IMF, many of them several times.

How many more crises do we need before humanity is willing to learn that this is a systemic issue, and that only structural changes will avoid repeating the same patterns? (A full inventory of the options on how to deal with a systemic banking crisis has been explained in another paper, by Lietaer, Ulanowicz & Goerner.[11])

A Structural Monetary Solution

Conventional economic thinking assumes the de facto monopolies of national currencies are an entirely natural phenomena. But the clear lesson from nature is that systemic monetary sustainability requires a diversity of currency systems, so that multiple and more diverse agents and channels of monetary links and exchanges can emerge.

It is important to realize that there are other ways to get back towards the Window of Viability; a total crash can be avoided. Solutions lie in letting complementary currency systems grow, or even encourage the soundest of them to blossom, and gradually and gently push back the excesses of the monoculture.

Conventional economists are correct when they claim that a diversity of media of exchange is less efficient than a monopoly. However, it has now been proven that complementary currencies facilitate transactions that otherwise wouldn't occur, linking otherwise unused resources to unmet needs, and encouraging diversity and interconnections that otherwise wouldn't exist. While this may result in a drop in efficiency, it is the necessary cost for increasing the resilience of the economic system.

At the other extreme, some complementary currency enthusiasts claim that we should encourage very large numbers of complementary currency systems, to the extent of letting everyone issue his or her own currency. At a certain point, of course, this scenario risks overshooting the Window of Viability in the other direction, producing stagnation.

It is very encouraging that at least one Central Bank has officially concluded that social currencies are not a threat to monetary policy, but actually contribute to the building of social capital and to the reduction of poverty.[12] Furthermore, we now also have empirical proof from 75 years of data from the WIR system in Switzerland that business-to-business complementary currencies tend to be counter-cyclical with the business cycle of conventional money: they actually help Central Banks in their task of stabilizing the national economy in terms of employment and in smoothing the swings in the business cycle.[13] In a period when unemployment, poverty and economic exclusion are all increasing in the developed world, it would be important that Central Banks revisit this issue with a more open mind than has been the case so far.

Policy Implications

Ironically, our financial system has become so fragile because it has become too efficient.

To achieve high efficiency, our modern monetary system has become too streamlined via a monoculture of a single type of money – a monoculture legally imposed in the name of market efficiency. Furthermore, governments enforce this monopoly by requiring that all taxes be paid exclusively in this particular type of currency.

We argue that making the monetary system sustainable will require a new balance between efficiency and resilience in economics, in a way similar to what occurs naturally in ecosystems. Humanity has become, involuntarily and reluctantly, the steward of this planet's biosphere. Ultimately, we have no choice but to learn how to make our global civilization sustainable, or it will cease to exist. It may be useful to remember here that Albert Einstein defined insanity as doing the same thing over and over again and expecting different results.

Next Steps?

What then should governments do to implement the approach proposed here? It could start by accepting other types of currencies, besides conventional bank-debt national money, for the payment of fees and taxes. For instance, the province of Vorarlberg, Austria, or the city of Bristol, in the UK, are now accepting specific complementary currencies in addition to conventional national money in payment of local taxes.

The trillion-dollar question facing us today is: How many more banking and monetary crashes do we have to live through before we have the humility to learn from complex natural systems? Could it be that governments may have to learn from the next crisis that they can't afford to save the banking system?

Bernard Lietaer has studied and worked in the field of money and payment systems for more than 30 years in an unusually broad range of capacities including Central Banker, fund manager, university professor, and a consultant to governments in numerous countries, multinational corporations, and community organizations. He co-designed and implemented the ECU, the convergence mechanism to the single European currency system (the Euro); and served as president of the Electronic Payment System while at the Belgian Central Bank. He is Research Fellow at the Center for Sustainable Resources at the University of California at Berkeley, and Professor in the Erasmus Mundus program at the Sorbonne in Paris. Information about his work is available on www.lietaer.com.

Notes

[1] Rösl, Gerhard, "Regional Currencies in Germany: Local Competition for the Euro?" Discussion Paper, Series 1: Economic Studies, No. 43/2006 (Deutsche Bundesbank Eurosystem, 2006). Available for download at http://www.bundesbank.de/download/volkswirtschaft/dkp/2006/200643dkp_en.pdf.

[2] Ulanowicz, Robert E., *A Third Window: Natural Life Beyond Newton and Darwin.* (West Conshohocken, PA: Templeton Foundation Press, 2009).

[3] Conrad, Michael, *Adaptability: The Significance of Variability from Molecule to Ecosystem.* (New York, Plenum Press, 1983).

[4] Odum, Eugene. P., *Fundamentals of Ecology* (Philadelphia: Saunders, 1953).

[5] Ulanowicz, Robert. E., Sally J. Goerner, Bernard Lietaer and Rocio Gomez, "Quantifying sustainability: Resilience, Efficiency and the Return of Information Theory," *Ecological Complexity* 6(1) (2009), pp. 27-36.

[6] Molly Dwyer, "Complexity and the Emergent Feminine: A Cosmological Inquiry into the Role of the Feminine in the Evolution of the Universe" (Winning Paper of the 1999 Vickers Award International Society for the Systems Sciences, Asimolar, California).

[7] Daly, Herman. E., *Beyond Growth: The Economics of Sustainable Development.* (Boston, Beacon, 1997).

[8] Friedman, Milton, "The Case for Flexible Exchange Rates," in *Essays in Positive Economics* (Chicago: University of Chicago Press, 1953), pp. 157-203.

[9] Keynes, John Maynard, *The General Theory of Employment, Interest and Money* (London: Macmillan, 1936), p. 159.

[10] Caprio, Gerard Jr, and Daniela Klingebiel, "Bank Insolvencies: Cross Country Experience," Policy Research Working Papers No. 1620 (Washington, DC, World Bank, Policy and Research Department, 1996); and Laevan, Luc and Fabian Valencia, "Resolution of Banking Crises: The Good, the Bad, and the Ugly," IMF Working Paper 10/146 (Washington: International Monetary Fund, 2010).

[11] Lietaer, Bernard, Robert E. Ulanowicz, and Sally J. Goerner, "Options for Managing a Systemic Bank Crisis," *Sapiens*, 2(1) (2009). Available online at http://sapiens.revues.org/ index747.html.

[12] Freire Vasconcellos, Marusa, "Social Economy and Central Banks: Legal and Regulatory Issues on Social Currencies (social money) as a Public Policy Consistent with Monetary Policy," *International Journal of Community Currency Research*, (Vol. 13, 2009), pp.76 – 94.

[13] Stodder, James, "Corporate Barter and Economic Stabilization," *International Journal of Community Currency Research*, 2 (1998); Stodder, James, "Reciprocal Exchange Networks: Implications for Macroeconomic Stability," Conference Proceedings, International Electronic and Electrical Engineering (IEEE), Engineering Management Society (EMS) (Albuquerque, New Mexico, 2000). Available for download at http://www.appropriateeconomics.org/materials/reciprocal_exchange_networks.pdf. An updated version (2005) is available at http://www.rh.edu/~stodder/Stodder_WIR3.htm; and Stodder, James, "Complementary Credit Networks and Macroeconomic Stability: Switzerland's Wirtschaftsring," *Journal of Economic Behavior and Organization*, 72, 79–95 (2009). Available for download at http://www.rh.edu/~stodder/BE/WIR_Update.pdf

Chapter 8

Africa, Digital Identity and
the Beginning of the End for Coins

By Jonathan Ledgard

DIGITAL IDENTITY WILL BE ONE OF the most significant philosophical, political and economic questions of the early 21st century. While this question will be a pressing one in richer countries, it will be absolutely vital in poorer ones where the state is often weak or absent and where mobile-accessed Internet will be the portal to new forms of education, health and banking.

Picture the connectivity in poor countries a few years hence as seen on the battered screen of a cheap (but fast) smartphone. How do you make sense of yourself when you enter in? Do you have rights? Who is directing the choices you make inside there, who is recording them, who profits from your explorations? Are you trammeled again and again to the same domains? Are you even a citizen anymore when you are online?

In Africa, by 2020, 200 million young people will come online for the first time. They will do so through the battered screens mentioned above, but also through new forms of tablets and wearable devices. These young Africans will be in a much stronger position to improve the quality of their lives if they are offered authentic and secure digital identities that allow them to control their own data and more easily move value among the various participants in peer-to-peer networks.

The latest demographic predictions suggest that fertility in Africa is not slowing. The continent's population may now reach 2.7 billion before 2050 – up from 230 million in 1950. By the end of the century the PIN code for the planet will be 1145: 1 billion for the Americas, 1 billion for Europe, 4 billion for Africa and 5 billion for Asia. Because of a lack of indigenous tech companies and the prevalence of English, French and Arabic as online languages, Africa will be a long-term play for big tech companies.

But by buying up so much digital real estate in Africa so cheaply they will likely achieve monopolistic positions; at some point in the early 2020s African users will find that nearly all their online interactions will be dominated by just a few companies – including Google, Facebook, Yahoo, Microsoft, and rising Asian giants like Samsung and Huawei. Throughout Africa they will run the computing architectures of user desktops, the civil service, stock exchanges and civil aviation. As smartphones and other sensors generate an explosion of data, African governments – erratic at best in the writing and implementing of laws governing data – are not likely to be at the forefront of security, privacy and consumer protections. By default, large tech companies will assume ever-more powerful positions versus the user – more powerful in many respects than governments themselves.

Despite steady improvements in connectivity in Africa with the laying of undersea cables, the online experience is likely to be patchy and expensive relative to the rest of the planet. The virginal moment for young Africans will likely be with Facebook, which has subsidized data charges to ramp up usage in many African markets. Facebook says it wants to massively increase access to the Internet in Africa as a common good, but it undoubtedly also has an eye on the burgeoning demographics. Even so, Facebook will be much smaller than Google. The Mountain View giant has beneficent and ingenious schemes of its own in Africa, such as the Loon project to improve Internet connectivity from balloons drifting at high altitudes. Such initiatives by big tech companies to provide email, software, search, mapping and data storage at a massive scale are welcome indeed.

It is in this context that the question of digital identity for young Africans becomes imperative. Where the state is weak and sometimes predatory, and where tech companies are overly dominant, it makes sense to push for a new trust layer that would retain data and build up a secure and authentic digital identity for every African who wants one. India's Aadhaar national identity scheme shows what is possible. It has already registered 500 million Indians using a number code and matching biometrics. Aadhar is improving service delivery, but it is strengthening the state in a way that tempts overreach.

Advances in distributed computing make it possible to think more audaciously in Africa. Instead of just tagging a citizen, why not gift them full digital sovereignty? Providing Africans with secure, reliable digital identities will greatly empower them to take charge of their own commercial, political and social affairs, especially over and against the interests of corrupt governments and large corporations.

An open source "white label" software built as standard into every smartphone, tablet and wearable device would allow Africans to access the power of the Internet on fairer terms. They could trade data for services, choose new providers that disrupt the big tech companies, or hold onto their own data as an asset for microloans. Providing each user with a personal data store using the "trusted compute cell architecture" would make it harder for big tech companies to scrape private information for their own ends. (For more, see Chapter 13, "The ID3 Open Mustard Seed Platform," by Thomas Hardjono et al.)

Such an offering would have to prove that it is robust enough to resist attack or theft of identity. The costs involved would be more difficult to handle. Who would pay for so many personal data stores? These are difficult but solvable problems. Costs are likely to fall as clean energy comes online and as Africa begins to benefit from cognitive computing and cables and other infrastructure improvements. For example, the architecture built to handle the enormous amounts of data that will be generated by the Square Kilometre Array radiotelescopy project under construction in South Africa's Kalahari desert, will have many spinoff benefits.

One of the first effects of user-controlled digital identity will be to alter the way value is moved around in Africa. Savings clubs are popular across Africa. Each month members pay into a pot, which is then reinvested. A digital identity solution may allow such clubs to negotiate collective deals much more effectively; in effect, to set up lucrative microeconomies. From there it is a short hop to launching viable digital currencies. Even the best economic scenarios suggest that the average wage in Africa will not exceed US$6 a day by 2030. In our lifetimes the vast majority of transactions in Africa will therefore be very small, such as the expenditures of pennies to use a latrine in a slum.

How are these transactions paid right now? Nearly always with coins and small denomination notes, and with no transaction records. Coins are a blunt instrument for carrying out these kind of tiny payments: many are lost, many lose their value, they are expensive to keep in circulation, and, besides, are grubby with pathogens.

A digital identity allows value to flow in new ways and therefore to enable all sorts of microtransactions. A digital identity as maintained by smartphones could start to replace coins and small denomination banknotes. As wearable technologies improve over the next decade it will become possible to imagine that many transactions will be consummated by gestures or by bursts of song; a bracelet raised, value imparted, precisely, with almost no transaction cost.

Cryptocurrencies like Bitcoin and Ripple have a headstart, but a pan-African digital currency could be index-based like Ven. In any case, a common African digital currency aimed at improving the value of low-value transactions may perversely help regional integration. Because of the peer-to-peer nature of the transactions it is possible to imagine localized versions – one for every great African city, certainly, but perhaps one for women here, for farmers there, and for Catholics everywhere. The design of the currency should be memorable; I propose a pronking impala to match the iconic springbok on the kruggerand.

An "Impala" revolution could provide a boost to Africa in a period of scarce jobs, expensive food and widespread destruction of nature. Mobile money schemes such as Kenya's M-Pesa have rightly been praised, but they are better suited for paying school fees or church tithes than for paying for a ripe banana. They do not work hard enough for the user.

By contrast, an Impala currency will set enforceable standards of performance and transparency. It could help users build credit histories to secure microloans for schooling, healthcare and housing. Governments and aid agencies using their own versions of the currency will have verifiable means of disbursing value accurately, cheaply, and in daily increments that might protect beneficiaries who would otherwise be exploited. Indeed, just as some African governments are promising laptops and tablets, so they might consider subsidizing wearable devices that boost inclusivity.

Since virtual transactions will happen mostly in the informal sector, African governments will lose little by setting a tax-free ceiling of a few dollars a day for every user. Taxes could trigger as a levy in an automatic exchange into a national currency when holdings of "Impala" exceed an agreed ceiling.

Jonathan Ledgard is Director, Future Africa, at the Swiss Federal Institute of Technology, and Africa correspondent-at-large of The Economist. *He has reported from 50 countries and several wars for* The Economist, *with a focus on politics, security, environment, and science, and has published two acclaimed novels,* Giraffe *(2007) and* Submergence *(2013).*

Chapter 9

Ven and the Nature of Money

By Stan Stalnaker

MONEY, BY ITS VERY NATURE, IS controversial. It goes hand in hand with power, and for centuries has been integral to the operative status of the nation-state system. It can be used to control and to guide, to redeem and to oppress: like any tool in the hands of humans. At its essence, money is a ledger, a system used by society to keep score of who and what and when and where. Money is our way of recording distributed memory.

The evolution of money is therefore very important, and as technology affects this part of the human experience as it has so many others, the principles and standards by which we blend technology and money together will have far-reaching consequences.

Hub Culture is a social network that has been exploring the convergence of technology and money for more than a decade. This very international community grew from a book of the same name, published in 2002. As a community its hallmarks are similar to others – collections of people with individual interests finding common ground in philosophy and experience. The community came before the currency and remains the anchor and the glue for the existence of Ven, its *raison d'etre*. The Hub Culture community, global in geography but singular in concept, discovered that the constraints of physical money – fiat currency – has distinct limitations for internationally minded people in meeting local needs, and from this constraint Ven was born. Today, the currency represents an innovative step forward in finance that combines technological excellence with community values: environmental respect, community responsibility, and self-sovereignty with distributed, selective privacy.

As the first widely used digital currency and now an Internet Reserve Currency, Ven's history is one of constant evolution. It first appeared in July 2007 as an application on Facebook. It had no real exchange rate and was traded as a type of digital karma between members. No one knew what it was worth, which made trade arbitrary and unwieldy. This lack of clear value did not last long, however. An exchange rate of 10 to 1 was created, linking Ven to the US Dollar. With a set value, Ven were first used inside Hub Culture stores – Hub Pavilions – worldwide, and could be traded among members on a global basis for free.

To mitigate exchange rate risks, the currency was diversified in 2009 to enable exchange with a basket of currencies, making it highly stable. The decision was also taken to back issuance of Ven 100% with assets, in accordance with the algorithmic index that formulated the Ven. Soon this basket of assets included commodities like gold and silver, and later, carbon, making Ven the first environmentally linked currency in the world.

With its stable, diversified backing and conservative structure, Ven suddenly showed promise as a global currency. But it was the introduction of carbon to the underlying basket of assets that gave Ven a "social DNA," embedding environmental support in every transaction as a derivative benefit. The more Ven circulating in the world, the more carbon purchased for asset reserves, and the more trees and habitats protected.

Today over 25,000 acres of Amazon rainforest have been put under protection, and Ven is developing funding protection programs in places as diverse as Costa Rica, Alaska and eastern Africa. There are multiple community benefits from this protection work – new wildlife corridors, natural preservation, fuel switching from charcoal to clean energy, and an increased quality of life for citizens of a very stressed planet.

Ven is rapidly scaling into the global financial system, becoming the first digital currency used for commodity trades, the first traded in regulated foreign exchange markets, and the first to enter bond markets and national bourses. It is the most stable currency in the world, roughly 50% less volatile than traditional fiat currencies. With no leverage and no interest, it fulfills some important aspects of Islamic finance. These attributes make Ven a yawn for speculators and cowboys, but a boon for producers and common people.

Ven is issued and regulated by Hub Culture and the Ven Central Reserve Board, a group of financial experts from within the community tasked with protecting the integrity of Ven. Ven and Hub Culture are protected in a legal Trust with the sole task of protecting the technological assets and intellectual property that governs the community. "Digital" means that the currency does not have physical representation and its distribution, flow and exchange are recorded on the Internet. The Ven Central Authority oversees policies governing Ven.

This is a markedly different strategy than the hundreds of decentralized cryptocurrencies that place their faith in a fixed supply of their currencies and reject central authorities to manage them. While decentralized currencies have their merit, the human role in managing Ven is designed to allow flexibility to deal with changing circumstances.

Governing rules regarding Ven provide simple fixed conditions: a social contract with users to assure a strict correspondence between Ven in circulation and asset reserves, and built-in support for the environment, to promote stability, reliability and security. Together these attributes support the Four Core Attributes of Ven: stability, globality, security and support for nature.

Ven Authorities

In order to make Ven more accessible, Hub Culture authorizes independent entities known as "Authorities" to manage the liquidity of Ven. Organizations may acquire this status for various purposes. For example, a bank would typically operate accounts on behalf of their customers. A currency exchange would be doing real-time currency trading. An NGO might issue relief aid or microfinance support. A corporation might convert assets to Ven to hedge their balance sheet or to meet carbon obligations. An investment fund might use authority status to hold and control large amount of Ven for a stable long-term investment solution.

Regular users and merchants who have only one account and do not use large volumes of Ven do not need Authority status. Authority status comes with a legal responsibility to make sure that all Ven activities are legal and ethical. Through those principles Hub Culture ensures Ven availability to anyone through any means while remaining a legal, stable, 100% backed asset acknowledged and respected worldwide.

Ven Issuance

Ven is held in the Glacier, an offline "cold" cryptovault. When purchased, Ven "melts" from the Glacier into circulation, and the corresponding purchase value in fiat currency is held in reserves allocated to the underlying basis components of Ven. Ven is a currency backed by a collection of other currencies, commodities and carbon credits. Technically this means for every Ven in a member account there are corresponding frozen assets held in reserve. This ensures the stability of Ven prices but also means that all Ven must be accounted for and backed in the Central Ven Reserve.

Ven is distributed through Authorities. If you access an Authority to buy Ven for $100, this amount is broken down and invested into dollars, euros, pounds, yen, yuan and many other currencies, commodities and carbon credits. When you sell Ven the underlying assets are released. This process is called Reserve Balancing. The process is managed through a series of sophisticated hedging algorithms that balance the underlying reserves and issuance in real time with live financial markets data, updating as frequently as several times per second.

Ven Pricing API

Ven pricing is updated in real-time and slightly fluctuates depending on underlying performance. Hub Culture makes Ven prices publicly available to anyone through an API, however this free public API is updated only once per hour. As an Authority, entities have access to high-frequency pricing which offers real-time pricing with precision of more than 0.1 second, to ensure that Authorities have a very accurate pricing before during and after purchase or sale. VEN purchase/sales orders can also be distributed through FIX protocol, which is popular among financial institutions worldwide.

Ven Authentication and HubID

As Ven moves into the financial markets and becomes more usable for purchases and transactions, the need to authenticate identity to avoid money laundering and other fraud risks becomes paramount. Since Ven issuance and exchange comes from a central point, and since it grew from the social network, an intrinsic layer of identity already exists with transactions.

However, the data sets generated by a centralized digital ledger imply unique challenges of their own because Ven users and Hub Culture certainly do not want transactional and personal data routinely made available to third parties. Uniquely among all social networks and most advertising-oriented social media, Hub Culture does not scrape, aggregate or sell member data to monetize it. In fact, not a single piece of user data has ever been sold to a third party – Hub Culture explicitly grants users unique ownership of their data within Hub Culture, their transaction data, and the Ven in their account. This can be done in theory with the data in the archives and in practice by passing ownership of decisions regarding the use of data to each member directly.

Such a system could not be practical or sustainable unless digital currency accounts are linked to profiles and costs are covered in other novel ways. For example, Hub Culture pioneered the concept of individual payments for content generated inside the network, through news and video posted by members – an opportunity made possible by individual data ownership. There are also "collaboration hubs" linked to private Ven accounts and even knowledge brokerage and retail opportunities – all of which feature margins.

In 2013, Hub Culture and M.I.T. Media Lab partnered with ID3 to take this idea to a radical next step: ensuring digital "self-sovereignty" with user data through the creation of HubID, a secure vault wrapped in elliptical curve cryptography and the Open Mustard Seed open source technology platform. Through this innovative blend of technologies, online users not only have a "Personal Data Store" (PDS) to put their personal data in perpetuity, they receive a unique piece of online real estate through a private "virtual machine" dedicated to hosting just their data. While Hub Culture currently covers the cost of that privilege, the growth of Ven redemption and usage will eventually overtake the costs of this service, enabling members to decide how and when data in their vault is used.

Data in the vault is segmented into a series of tabs, each of which are designated a unique hex color on the Web. These tabs combine to form the HubID, a digital badge that manifests these verified components with the member's profile image. Together, these elements form a unique Aura, which can be accessed by others who desire to authenticate a user transaction with Ven. The final result is a digital identity and transaction capability owned by the individual and uniquely verified. At the core of this technology is voice biometric technology developed with Validsoft, a leading mobile security firm, to provide near-perfect uniqueness in digital identity for highly secure access and transaction approvals.

Together, HubID and Ven seek to provide a completely intelligent, self-sovereign Web experience. The technology works with all other systems, granting a unique API for identity to each user, which can be adapted and used only with the member's approval. At their discretion, users often pay for, or receive payment for, access privileges in Ven.

This technology is the basis for Voin, an intelligent data coin now in development by Hub Culture. Voin is the world's first intelligent coin, and can slip into a pocket, hang from a chain around the neck, or rest on a lapel. With fingerprint and voice biometric technology it is highly secure, but also easy to use: the owner simply speaks a value into Voin and matches a voiceprint for access to make a transaction. As both a transaction wallet and an ID, Voin represents a completely new approach to money and the application of closed loop device payments.

At Hub Culture, the belief is that an increasingly connected world should provide greater data transparency and equality. It should also be more secure, with individual privacy and personal data control included as an indelible human right. The general drift of businesses in the Internet age has been toward winner-take-all scenarios and the total, one-way vacuum suck of data aggregation. This is having dramatic (negative) consequences in a sector as important as ubiquitous value exchange because information and value are merging at the same time that chokepoints in the system are narrowing. If individuals are not given control and ownership of this data now, they risk losing it forever.

Technological innovations are giving the world a rich opportunity to rethink the values around the economy without having to compromise on the practical, hard-nosed financial realities of commerce. A properly managed nonfiat digital currency has some inherent advantages over a state-based currency: it can function at one degree of separation from the state, and without the baggage of obligations that states must shoulder, such as the need to provide defense, fund social services and build and repair public works. While limitations around taxation and use of force mean that digital currencies will never fully replace fiat currencies, their advantages do not absolve them from adhering to some form of social contract with their users.

The nature of money is to reflect and strengthen the values of the community in which it operates. If a currency does not do this, it fails in the most important test of its moral existence, and over time can never reach full potential. Digital currencies like Ven provide great technological efficiencies, ease of use, stability and more, but Ven's most important attribute is its philosophy that humans should play a defining role in monetary policy and that including externalities in the DNA of currency can radically improve the welfare of the communities that use it. After all, isn't that what money is for?

Stan Stalnaker *is Founding Director, Hub Culture and Ven Currency and Communications Chair for the Digital Asset Transfer Authority, the industry's self-regulatory organization. A leading commentator on the social impact of globalization, emergence of digital asset classes, P2P economies and of course digital currency, he is putting his undergraduate economics and international development degrees to more use than he or his professors ever thought possible.*

Chapter 10

Green Coins: Using Digital Currency to Build the New Power Platform

By Reed E. Hundt, Jeffrey Schub and Joseph R. Schottenfeld

THE SOFTWARE BREAKTHROUGHS THAT HAVE MADE possible Bitcoin – the new cryptocurrency, regardless of how the IRS chooses to treat it – also can be used for almost any widespread and equitable sharing of a scarce resource. That's why the authors, working through a non-profit called the Coalition for Green Capital[1] are exploring ways to link the new software capabilities with distributed solar power. We hope that building owners will not only put solar panels on their own roofs to self-provide power, but also will share that power with each other, using the software behind Bitcoin to enable fair payments to each rooftop power generator.

Today, rooftop solar accounts for an extremely small proportion of total electricity generation. In 2012, for instance, distributed solar generation made up only 0.2 percent of total retail sales of electricity in the United States.[2] But, the federal and state governments provide very large subsidies for solar power. Federal incentives may be worth more than 55 percent of the total cost, and state level incentives can be worth another 25 percent, meaning the system owner may have to shoulder only 20 percent of the actual cost of solar.[3] Here follows an example of the simplest structure of a rooftop solar purchase.

The sun indubitably can provide all the energy needed by the global economy.[4] Technologists have been rapidly advancing the capability to convert the sun's rays into electricity, and efficiency gains have been accelerating. Furthermore, due to rising supply, especially out of China, panel costs have been dropping very rapidly. Moreover,

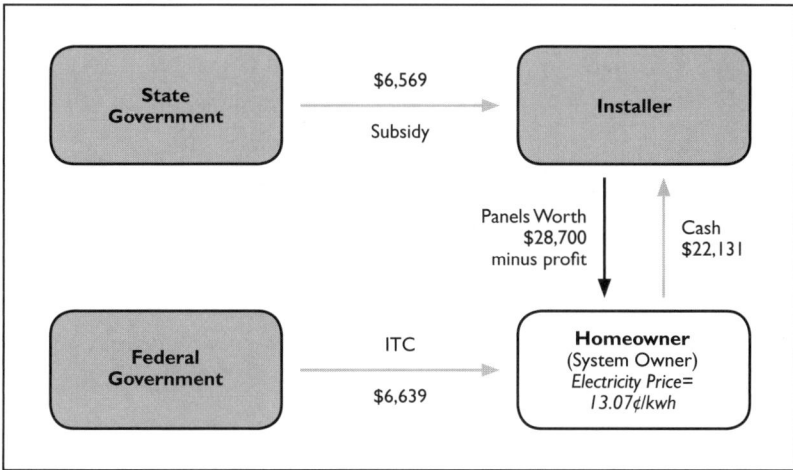

Fig. 1: Typical Cash Purchase for Solar

rooftops beckon for panels – there is no important competing use for the space; installation is easy; and the business creates jobs for which skills are abundant and underutilized. Last year, solar power created jobs in nearly every state.[5]

Scaling distributed solar faces two distinct problems. First, installers and government currently treat distributed solar as a benefit solely for the owner of a particular rooftop. There is little or no community or group-based demand for solar power. Second, by thinking of rooftop solar as a power source for the specific underlying home and not as a communitywide resource, homeowners and installers are not maximizing the amount of panels and power generation that could be obtained from a given home's roof.

To solve these two problems, we are looking for creative ways to encourage widely distributed rooftop owners to install solar panels and supply solar power both to each other and to other users. They must use the electric grid to connect, of course, but if the group is big enough, it can muster the resources to negotiate a low transmission price from the grid owner. These individuals would need a way to connect – preferably with the option to maintain their anonymity – and their connections would need to allow for constant updating of the account of each rooftop owner. As additional rooftops are added to the group, the capability of the whole system would increase by

more than the marginal increments of power added by each new solar provider. A larger number of scattered users creates a smoother,
more continuous pattern of power generation. It also provides a
greater capacity to offset the variable bursts of consumption and dips
in production by each individual rooftop owner.

With these dynamics in mind, we are exploring how the introduction and adaptation of a block chain, the decentralized ledger
that tracks and certifies all transactions of Bitcoin, and a solar cryptocurrency might be used by a community of solar rooftop owners.
A decentralized, disaggregated ledger-powered currency could be
converted to renewable energy credits and other government-driven
subsidies. It could even serve as a medium of exchange within solar
microgrids or networks, and the network effects created by a robust
ecosystem of green currency could organically drive adoption.

Solar ledgers could help assure participants that their electricity use and generation can both remain anonymous. The protocols
behind a cryptocurrency like Bitcoin would allow for transactions
between users, but not require actual identification of any rooftop
owner. Moreover, the absence or near absence of transaction costs
and the speed of processing would permit the constant flow of transactions that a network of solar users would need to operate successfully.

Since the introduction of Bitcoin in 2008 by a pseudonymous
programmer named Satoshi Nakomoto, cryptocurrencies and "block
chains" have provoked significant controversy. Cyberlibertarians
praise cryptocurrencies as the end of centralized banking; small business owners look forward to a future when cryptocurrencies will allow them to bypass bank processing fees; law enforcement fears that
drug traffickers will use bitcoins to transact drug deals on black market websites such as the Silk Road. Last month, news that Mt. Gox,
the largest Bitcoin exchange house, had lost nearly US$500 million
worth of bitcoins promptly caused the currency's value to halve.[6]
Driven by speculation, bitcoins' value is volatile, even in the absence
of Mt. Gox-like shocks. With good reason, many wonder about the
real worth of fiat-less cryptocurrencies or coins generated by code

and "mined" by using computing power to make increasingly complex proof-of-work calculations. (This is especially disturbing because the amount of electricity and computing power now needed to mine bitcoins has an enormous carbon footprint.[7])

Nevertheless the promise of a distributed ledger and cryptocurrency is very great for distributed solar generation. The ability for one individual, group or entity to transfer funds directly to another, with the community (the miners) digitally verifying the transaction in the place of a third party (generally a bank) has nearly limitless potential. [8] Positive uses of block chains enabling currencies or commodities are already proliferating. Donors used dogecoin, originally viewed as a meme-based spoof of Bitcoin, to fund the Jamaican bobsled team's appearance at the Sochi Winter Olympics. More recently, an anonymous user moved more than US$10,000 worth of dogecoins through Twitter – the largest donation ever made by tweet – to fund clean water projects.[9] Developers and programmers are creating entirely new cryptocurrencies aimed at providing social benefits: Gridcoin, for example, rewards miners for donating computing power to the Berkeley Open Infrastructure Network Computing Grid, which employs a global, decentralized network of computers to conduct scientific computing.[10]

SolarCoin has begun to explore how the concept of a cryptocurrency could be adapted to incentivize solar. Introduced in February 2014 by a group of volunteers associated with The SolarCoin Foundation, SolarCoin promotes solar adoption by creating an added motivation to produce solar power: in addition to renewable energy credits and other government subsidies that individuals already receive, solar producers would receive one SolarCoin for every megawatt hour (MWh) of energy produced.[11]

Unlike Bitcoin, SolarCoins are not, strictly speaking, fiat-less. Their value derives from the generation of solar power, which has some demonstrable economic value. Rather than only using computing power to demonstrate proof-of-work solutions and thereby mint new coins ("mining"), users can also earn new coins by producing more solar power. The more power produced, the greater the quantity of SolarCoin introduced into circulation. The open source code promises an equitable distribution between coins rewarded for cryptographic mining and coins earned through verified metered readings of solar electricity generation.

Of course, the coins have no intrinsic value. For now, earning a SolarCoin equates to little more than receiving a certificate of appreciation – a valueless acknowledgment. Over time, the coin's founders hope that a community of interest will help create economic value for the coins: foundations and concerned parties could donate value as a means of rewarding others for purchasing solar panels and producing solar energy. Added value may derive from green businesses or solar-dependent businesses doing the same – out of altruism or to lower solar energy costs and increase their own margins. In the future, should the digital coins gain real monetary value, other vendors could pledge to accept the coins to boost their perceived social value.[12]

But there are other ways that a new solar cryptocurrency supported by a block chain could gain value and drive solar. By aggressively recruiting vendors to accept the currency or trade in it – rather than waiting for vendors to sign on – SolarCoin or a different solar cryptocurrency could gain value from its usability, such as the use of block chains in transactions between solar users. The block chain itself could become a kind of "fiber" connecting solar producers who want to be able to bargain directly with the grid or, over time, trade or move energy within the network of solar providers. Perhaps best of all, in a time of extreme data hunger, solar producers could do much of this while remaining pseudonymous for as long as they wish.

It will be a while before SolarCoin or something similar gains such widespread acceptance that people would consider using the currency to trade for energy credits or subsidies (or that the government would permit this to happen). A reasonable question to ask is why we are discussing our plans in this publication. The answer is that we are inviting collaboration. We want to figure out how to get there, and in the classic open source tradition, we believe that at least some of the readers of this volume will have crucial ideas and connections to help us reap the full potential of this vision. We can be contacted by emailing Jeffrey Schub at jeff@coalitionforgreencapital. com.

Reed E. Hundt *is the CEO of the Coalition for Green Capital, a nonprofit organization headquartered in Washington, D.C., that works to establish green banks at the state, federal and international levels. He is also the Principal of REH Advisers, a business advisory firm. He was Chairman of the Federal Communications Commission from 1993 to 1997. He sits on various corporate and nonprofit boards including Intel Corporation, and the Connecticut Clean Energy Finance and Investment Authority.*

Jeffrey Schub *is Vice President of the Coalition for Green Capital.*

Joseph R. Schottenfeld *is a research associate at REH Advisors and the Coalition for Green Capital.*

Notes

[1] http://www.coalitionforgreencapital.com.

[2] "Bernstein Commodities & Power: The Empire Strikes Back: How the U.S. Distributed Solar Revolution Could Be Nipped in the Bud," *Bernstein Research,* January 3, 2014.

[3] See http://www.dsireusa.org/solar.

[4] Tom Murphy, "Solar Data Treasure Trove," August 7, 2012, http://physics.ucsd. edu/do-the-math/2012/08/solar-data-treasure-trove/#more-1159.

[5] Katie Valentine, "90 Percent of States Added Solar Jobs in 2013, Fueled By Growth In the South," *Thinkprogress,* February 11, 2014, at http://thinkprogress. org/climate/2014/02/11/3279221/states-solar-jobs-2013.

[6] Rachel Abrams, Matthew Goldstein, and Hiroko Tabuchi, "Erosion of Faith Was Death Knell for Mt. Gox," *The New York Times,* February 28, 2014, available at http://dealbook.nytimes.com/2014/02/28/mt-gox-files-for-bankruptcy/?_php=true&_type=blogs&_r=0.

[7] Michael Carney, "Bitcoin Has a Dark Side: Its Carbon Footprint," *Pando Daily,* December 16, 2013, http://pando.com/2013/12/16/bitcoin-has-a-dark-side-its-carbon-footprint.

[8] Tom Simonite, "What Bitcoin Is, and Why It Matters," *M.I.T. Technology Review,* May 25, 2011, http://www.technologyreview.com/news/424091/what-bitcoin-is-and-why-it-matters.

[9] Rob Wile, "Anonymous Redditor Makes Massive $11,000 Dogecoin Donation on Twitter," *Business Insider,* March 17, 2014, http://www.businessinsider. com/11000-dogecoin-for-world-water-day-2014-3.

[10] See: http://www.gridcoin.us.

[11] See: http://solarcoin.org.

[12] Lauren C. Williams, "Could A Solar-Powered Currency Be The Next Bit-coin?" *Thinkprogress*, February 21, 2014, http://thinkprogress.org/climate/2014/02/21/3282131/solar-coin-global-currency.

Part III

OPEN ARCHITECTURES FOR AN OPEN SOCIETY

Chapter 11

Organic Governance Through the Logic of Holonic Systems

By Mihaela Ulieru

THE BIGGEST CHALLENGE MANKIND FACES TODAY is not the development of more breakthrough technology; it is to create a society whose institutions integrate the knowledge that must precede any such technology, including knowledge about these institutions themselves. The inherent problem stems from our limited capacity to comprehend the interplay of large crowds of people and to transcend our own individual psychology rooted in interactions with groups of tens to hundreds, not billions.[1]

There is no doubt that our world has evolved to be complex, a phenomenon that reflects the ultimate manifestation of self-organized structure embedded in the physics of everything as archetypes of naturally emerging design.[2] This tendency occurs because all of nature is not comprised of physical objects as such but rather as a complex of flow particles merging into systems that change and evolve their configurations over time. The interrelationships that govern flows tend to create greater access to the circulating forces, which in turn propels new complexity. Anybody who has participated in the phenomenon of viral social media understands this intuitively – namely, that there are characteristic ways that flows change their configuration over time to increase their flows more. Social systems adapt to demands that enhance or obstruct these natural flows, much as natural systems do, through gradual modification and selection.

So, in the quest to design institutions and organizations that can perform more flexibly and effectively, we need to focus on how to enhance creative flows via structures that afford higher degrees of freedom. For this, we find plenty of inspiration and guidance in nature and the Universe.

To overcome the significant challenge in learning how to organize our daily life together in groups whose interactions are larger and more complex than we can intuit, we have to design rules of conduct and incentives that align our individual actions with collective interests so that both converge and yield synergies. *Over a long enough timeframe, manmade designs can emerge and behave like natural flow systems. But the puzzling thing for us as humans in the modern world is the persistence of bad designs, of intractable configurations limiting freedoms that could improve flow.* The rigid structure of our social, political and economic systems tends to thwart adaptation and agile responses to unexpected and emerging needs. Our macro-institutions often block effective, necessary solutions.

A recurrent problem is our failure to understand that human endeavors are part of holistic, living systems, natural and constructed, whose constitutive elements are mutually defining, expressive and constantly evolving. In actual circumstances, the individual cannot be cast as against, below or above the group; the individual is in fact nested *within* dynamic forms of social organization. Living organisms have subjectivities, intersubjectivities and behaviors that are nested within larger living systems. The dynamic complexities rapidly multiply, outpacing simple cause-and-effect logic and crude narratives.

Holonics is an empirically based theory of living systems that seeks to overcome these limitations. By blending multiple scientific and humanistic disciplines, holonics seeks to understand the rules and laws of self-organizing systems and, in so doing, point to the ways by which we might change the cultures in our organizations and transform how we live and work. But this challenge requires that we consider a radical shift in the ways in which we interact with (and within) our socio-politico-economic systems, as well as with the natural environment.

Holonics: Healthy Hierarchies

At its broadest scope, holonics is concerned with the evolution of the universe.[3] The basic idea is that every living entity is both an autonomous whole unto itself as well as part of a larger holistic system. This perspective enables us to see certain recurring patterns of self-organization among interdependent natural systems at many different scales, from atomic levels to earthly physics, biology and ultimately to the Universe.

In the 1960s the writer Arthur Koestler postulated that many biological and social organizations simultaneously display part/whole relationships. In other words, every entity is self-contained while concurrently existing as an individual member of a larger collective. Koestler proposed the term *holon* to describe the elements of these systems. This term is a combination of the Greek word *holos*, meaning "whole," with the suffix *on* meaning "part," as in prot*on* or neur*on*. The term is meant to reflect the tendencies of holons to act as autonomous entities that also cooperate to form nested hierarchies of subsystems. The classic example is the nested hierarchy in biology of the cell, tissue, organ and system/organism. In this holarchy, as Koestler called it, each holon is a subsystem retaining the characteristic attributes of the whole system (Fig. 1a). What actually defines a holarchy is a *purpose* around which holons are clustered and subdivided in subholons, at several levels of resolution. Each entity (or *holon*) must act autonomously *and* cooperatively to achieve the goals of itself and of the wider system.

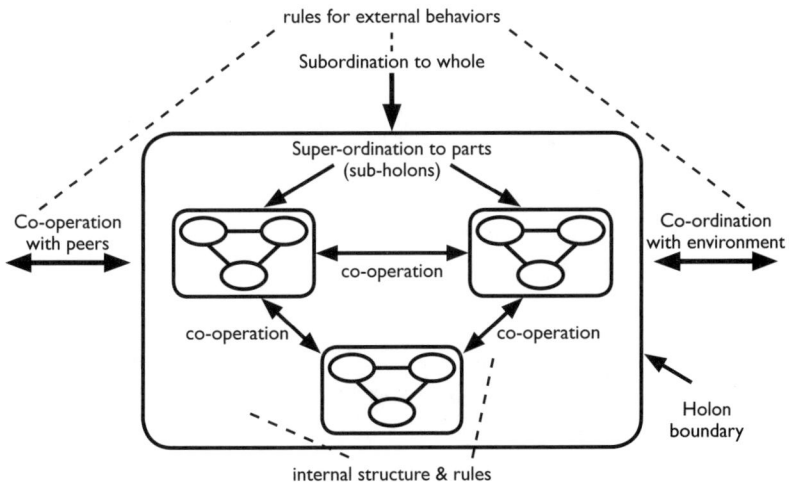

Fig.1a: Holarchy as a nested hierarchy

Top

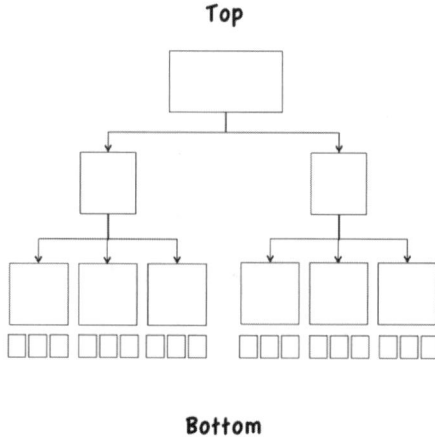

Bottom

Fig. 1b: Rigid (pathological) hierarchy

Holonics, then, is an *organizational paradigm* inspired by the self-organizing properties of natural systems. Holonics scales systems in nested clusters – as shown in Fig. 1a – whose collaborative rules drive them towards a *common purpose*. For example, a confederation is a *political holarchy* in which – at the highest level of resolution – the country and its governance rules (the federal government) are concerned with international politics and federal regulations. At the immediate lower level, there are provinces with their own set of governance rules that are concerned with things more appropriate to their scale, such as education and health matters. Finally at the "lowest" level in a nested hierarchy of confederation, there are cities with their municipal governance rules for such needs as snow removal and firefighting. Each citizen is an "individual agent" ("primitive" or "basic" holon) within this social holarchy.

Holarchies can take many forms.[4] For example, a university is organized as an *educational* holarchy comprised of the President's office, to which faculties (e.g., engineering, science, medicine, etc.) are directly subordinate to a dean's leadership; and each faculty in various departments (e.g., electrical engineering, manufacturing engineering, civil engineering, etc.) is subordinated in turn to the leadership of a department head. Each academic lecturer and each student is a primitive holon. An enterprise is a *purpose-driven/market-driven* holarchy. A manufacturing system is a *production-driven* holarchy. A living organism is a survival-driven holarchy. The Universe itself can be seen as an evolution-driven nested hierarchy, a holarchy. Hierarchies are ubiquitous in nature and social organization. But there are problematic hierarchies that we can designate as "pathological hierarchies." These are rigid, top-down, "tree-like" hierarchies (Fig. 1b), rather than holonic, nested hierarchies akin to nested Russian dolls (Fig. 1a). In pathological hierarchies, a "higher level top agent" (e.g., a university president or a manager of an organization) assumes the role of the whole and treats subsidiary systems as simple parts. Such higher level agents may use a coercive authority to micromanage the "lower" holons by issuing top-down instructions for each step of a process. This kind of pathological hierarchy can not only stifle human dignity, it can block the natural generative flows through which human creative potential manifests itself.

Unfortunately, such pathologies pervade our current entropic industrial order, in part because they rely upon reductive categories of thought and centralized forms of control that cannot flexibly align individual and collective interests. In a holonic system, by contrast, the autonomy of nested systems (at "lower levels") is recognized by allowing them to self-organize their own appropriate rules. Cooperation among interdependent parts in a holarchy (Fig. 1a) produces far more stable and effective results than traditional hierarchies (Fig. 1b) in which people are assigned rigid, constrained roles that underutilize their capacities.[5]

As this analysis suggests, it is important that we grasp the dynamics of holonic systems if we are going to change the pathologies of top-down approaches to organizational governance. It is possible to design agile systems that empower individuals to use their full capacities, but that will require a more holistic perspective of the interrelationships of holons and the flows that are enhanced (or blocked) by the respective individual-group dynamics.

The Logic of Holonic Systems:
Embracing the Individual *and* the Collective

The greatest challenge facing any holonic system is "the whole in the part" dichotomy, which can be understood as a set of built-in, contradictory tensions. Individual systems (wholes) holons are animated to be autonomous and separate – yet they are also constrained as parts of the holarchy to work cooperatively with other holons towards the common goal around which the holarchy was formed. This duality of contradictory forces within a holarchy – between autonomy and cooperation – is reconciled and balanced via "holonic design rules" that define the functionality of systems of semi-autonomous holons. The rules enable and "regulate" the flows through which subsystems can adapt to changing demands facing the holarchy when dealing with problem-rich environments. The rules thus endow the disparate holons with interdependence and an enduring coherence: in essence, the structural capacity of the holarchy to integrate its various parts. A crucial feature of the rules is their capacity to coordinate with the local environment – that is, with other holons and subholarchies.

A deeper dive into the inner workings of holonic systems reveals the mechanisms supporting this interdependence, which may be more familiar to us as "team spirit." The underlying feature is a "holonic logic" that balances autonomy and cooperation in the individual/group dynamics within the holarchy. As shown in Fig. 2, this logic must reconcile two equally foundational epistemologies: the *subject/subject* way of knowing (which arises through *participation*) and the *subject/object* way of knowing (which arises as individual agents interact with(in) heterogeneous social forms).[6]

The *subject/object way of knowing* is rooted in an individual's objectively verifiable observations of the world. For example the weight of a bag of groceries is objective because it can be put on a scale that every subject (individual) can read and conclude that it weighs, say, twelve pounds. It is practically impossible to relate to other individuals in this manner, since a person is much more than their precise weight or height; it is a complex conglomerate of subjectivities that cannot be perceived nor dealt with properly in such a reductionist manner. Such objectification not only prevents us from perceiving another individual in his or her wholeness, it obscures our own cognitive biases rooted in preconceptions, preferences, desires, etc. Unfortunately our Western culture favors the "objective" way of knowing, thus encouraging an impersonal, instrumental way of relating to others to satisfy one's narrow personal interests.

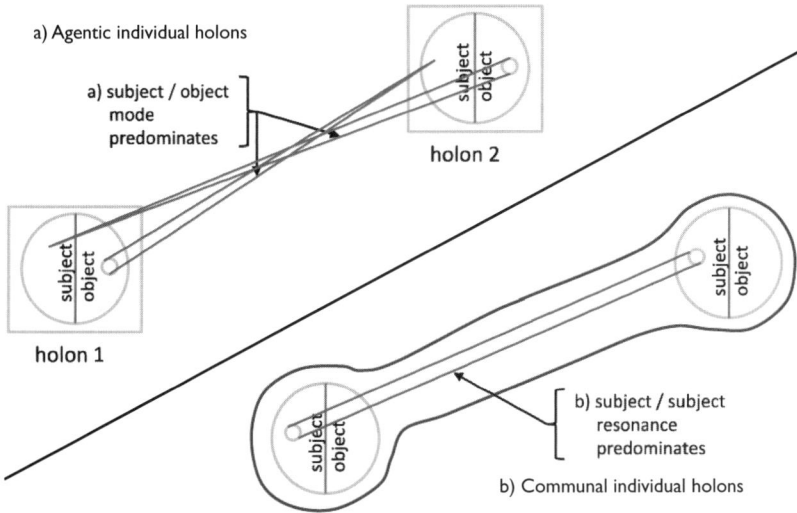

Fig.2: The two ways of relating in the holonic dyad

By contrast, the *subject/subject way of knowing* is rooted in an individual's subjective experiences of the world, which are private, internal events particular to the individual experiencing them. The bag of groceries that objectively weighs twelve pounds may feel subjectively lighter to an athlete but heavy to a frail, older person – or it might start to feel medium-heavy to someone after carrying it a few blocks and feel really heavy by the time she makes it home. Once we can acknowledge that perceiving other individuals (or elements of nature) is an inherently subjective challenge, we can realize that "the other" is *always* a richer, more complicated entity than our "objective" ways of knowing can encompass. Subject/subject knowing, then, is a way by which we can embrace and reclaim the "wholeness" of "other" individuals and nature.

As the individual develops from childhood to adulthood its individuality crystallizes against the forces of the group (family, peer pressure, societal norms, etc.) to which he/she applies the subject/object-based epistemological relation of two individual holons (Fig.

2a) that constitutes the basis of individual agency (and its social communion). This is necessary for the proper development of individual agency. However, once a person reaches adulthood, he or she becomes aware of the inherent subjectivity in everyone's cognition and with this capacity can begin to implicitly identify with "the other" in an empathic way – a connection called "subject/subject resonance" (Fig. 2b). This empathetic connection between two individual holons – to treat another as you would wish to be treated – constitutes the basis of individual communion with "another." The subject/subject resonance over time increases the social agency among a group, or what might be called the strength of "holonic togetherness."

By the terms of holonic logic, just as one individual cannot logically exist as a subject/object except in relation to another subject/object individual, so every individual is embedded by way of holonic resonance in a larger structural whole, the collective. This implies a dynamic, dialectical interplay of "individual mind" and "group mind." The agentic and communal poles of both individual holons and social holons blend in a kind of cross-dialectical model. (See Fig. 3.) The social holon exerts its agency through its cohesive structure, which applies a "counter-pressure" on the developing individual holon. This helps maintain the coherence and shared purpose of the social holon. At the same time, the social holon exhibits *communality* through its openness to other species and cultures. In human terms, this may consist of everything from intertribal mixes to culturally complex nation-states and now global culture.

The "world arises" in each moment as an individual in the subject/object mode of relating encounters "another" in a subject/object mode of relating (Fig. 3a). At the same time this evolves and unfolds in relation to the holonic togetherness that arises through the subject/subject resonance of group-mind and nature-field at every level (Fig. 3b). The psychologist routinely sees individuals struggling to integrate this "holonic dichotomy" – the need to develop individual agency over and against societal norms, that is, to differentiate themselves, while being integrated and "accepted" by the others at the same time (Fig. 3a). From another perspective, the sociologist sees societies as complex holons of individuals coming together through cultural paradigms, shared beliefs and narratives, and continuously evolving through each individual's own development (Fig. 3b).

The psychologist's view presumes an *agentic society* grounded in resonance and immediate commonality, while the sociologist's view presumes a communal society grounded in intentional agreements. Neither approach leads to the other: they are different (polar) ways of understanding the same world. But they are partial perspectives that holonics seeks to integrate. Holonic systems embrace in equal measure both the individual with its differentiated agency *and* the collective (the group/team, society, the state, etc.) on the same level (horizontally). This integration occurs on the same level because the collective does not constitute a *higher level* whole or a *separate environment* of which the individual is merely a part; the integration is a result of *both* individual agency and communion with the collective, reconciling their differences through the mechanisms of holonic interdependence – a kind of "synergistic togetherness" that blends the individual and the social.[7]

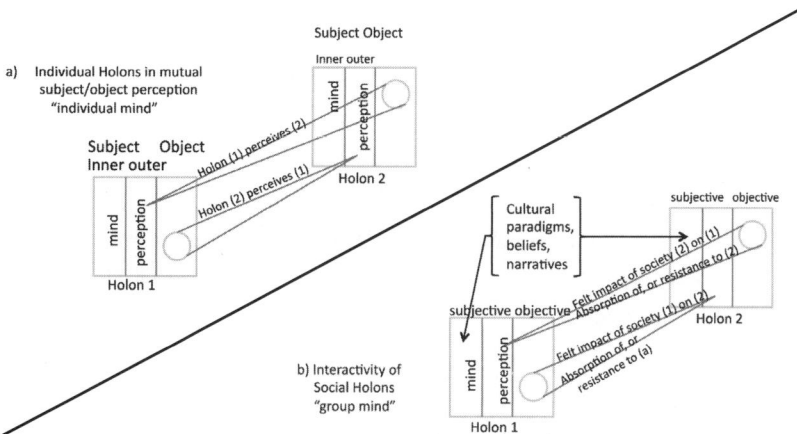

Fig.3: The two polar ways of understanding: a) "individual mind" and b) "group mind"

Most of the problems we face today stem from an overemphasis on the subject/object ways of relating to one another and to the world in general. This way of knowing and relating privileges individual agency and the propensity to build rigid individual hierarchies that do not take account of intersubjective cognition. An individual approaches "others" and the world from a solipsistic perspective and treats everything as subservient to individual wants and needs. At its extreme, this paradigm of beliefs and narratives manifests as the reductionist "man reigning over" nature and everything else in the Universe – a paradigm that has been disastrous in all areas of life, from climate change and energy crisis to societal and organizational governance.

However, as individual agency *and* communion move toward a balance, so do sociocultural agentic and communal ways of being and relating. As a society, we are now witnessing a shift away from maximal agentic individuality and social communion, toward an intensifying individual communion and social agency. The dialectical "either/or" which constitutes the familiar dualisms of subject/object, mind/matter, individual/social, and the cognitively dissonant "right/wrong," is beginning to move toward a new polarity of "both/and," which is characteristic of the subject/subject resonance. The subject/subject mode of knowing is becoming more deeply valued as we rediscover our place vis-à-vis each other as well as within nature and the Universe.

The time has come for us to step down from the top of our imaginary hierarchies to integrate ourselves within the larger whole(s), at the same level. This can only be achieved by approaching "other" and "nature" with empathy, which gives rise to a greater communal holonic resonance. This reorientation is key to redesigning societal rules that will turn us from selfish predators into altruistic, generative creators,[8] and to redefining our relationship to nature from scavengers to responsible caretakers. A new social agency begins to arise rooted in local group identity, which manifests through a culture of deep caring and understanding of "the other" from "the inside," approaching all living creatures, nature and the universe with the same desire for their well-being as we have for ourselves.

Reconceptualizing Social Change: Holonics as a Moral Choice

How can such insights help to change the societal game? The current set of rules, shaped and amplified by modern technology, essentially require business models based on increasing returns to scale (a scenario that classical economics deemed impossible). Contemporary rules also favor single winners with world-spanning power along with a diminishing circle of people controlling a greater and greater proportion of our society's wealth. Under these circumstances, markets, individual self-interest and libertarianism are incapable of solving societal and environmental problems because they are committed to the illusion that man occupies the top of a cosmic hierarchy and that power and politics are tools to enforce certain rules that favor "winners." This perspective is unable to encompass care about human beings in their wholeness, as can be actualized, for example, through the commons and by working together for the greater good. While Adam Smith may have theorized that the Invisible Hand would naturally and automatically yield the common good, his ideas were born in a society with pervasive social, political and legal constraints on individual license.

The challenge of our time is to embrace the reality of group interests and to devise governance systems that include those marginalized by elites who have commandeered "the system" to secure their economic authority. Collective provisioning, as in group health insurance, is not a state-based "socialism" but in holonic terms, a blending of the interests of the whole *and* of each and every individual. Having won the most significant battles against labor, companies and investors are now buying the electoral process – the very set of "governance rules" on which the "winners" thrive in our "pathological" society. It is time to change the rules with more inclusive and generative ones and embed them into constitutional systems that can enable free flows of creativity in trusted structures that are resistant to capture.

The great appeal of holonics is that it places societal communion at its core, giving the human spirit a chance to address our massive failure of social governance. With the *human* compound-holon that we know as society *and* as the individual, the logic of holonic systems offers a way to reconcile the two polarities of individual agency and social communion. Holonics insists that we recognize subjective experience as a legitimate domain of inquiry equivalent to the privileged objective domain of traditional science. At the same time it clarifies the logical, interconnected relations of individual and society.

Taking holonic principles seriously, however, requires a whole new mind – one that allows the range and diversity of our ontological narratives to continuously compose and decompose themselves. This new mind enables us to become participants in a persistent plurality of novel relationship that embraces differences and thrives on them. The incommensurability of beliefs that pervade our lives can serve as a source of generative novelty in a unified process of "shared becoming." Holonic principles invite us to move beyond the idea of separation and conflict, which are the only plausible ways for the dualistically constructed dialectical mind ("either/or" – "right/wrong") to resolve differences.

With the logic of holonic systems we can redesign our relationship and relatedness to others in the social web. It is possible to construct open, self-organizing fellowships of personal commitment and shared response-ability, in an intimate field of deep interpersonal relatedness and care. In this field of holonic resonance, we are better able to develop clear mind, right body and vital spirit with agency: our personal journey toward self-mastery.

But it is also evident that the greatest strength and power reside in social communion as the relational ground that unites each fellow into a more excellent whole. We can reimagine the design rules of our education, politics and business systems with a focus on discovery and wisdom. We can design processes that enrich the qualities of interdependent care, integrated development, and deeply shared trust that arise from basic human kindness and well-being. Generative transpersonal fields that reclaim both the individual and the collective are capable of transforming the world in powerful and extraordinary ways.

One result of cultivating generative transpersonal fields is that new sorts of creative clusters can self-organize in new, emergent ways. This can foster both human evolutionary development as well as technological development, producing unprecedented flows of local "socio-technical combinatorics."[9] (See Fig. 4.) Another result is a new emphasis on collective diversity over and against the forces of global homogenization, which dismisses the uniqueness and diversity of each individual. Having over-emphasized a "social communion" in which the individual is depleted of its "unique flavors," such homogenization has squandered the particular gifts and talents that each individual can contribute to the "whole" and thus the richness of the whole. By reclaiming the individual in its wholeness of "flavors," holonics unleashes this very richness of social agency into a new world order. The creative expression arising from every "group mind" can produce a synergetic blend of diversities (whether local or virtual) that can offer effective solutions to the challenges facing us while enriching the global tapestry of life on our planet.[10]

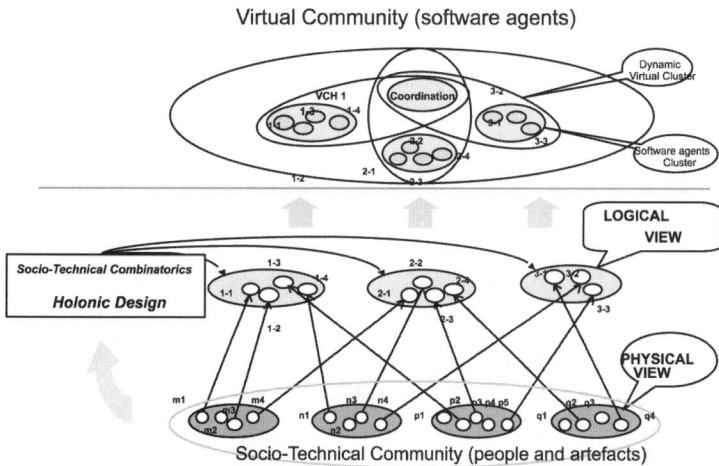

Fig. 4: Holonic Software Infrastructure

Holacracy: Holonic Design for Agile Organizational Governance

The types of interpersonal relations and authority that industrial organizations rely upon (entirely based on subject/object modes of interaction) naturally result in either competition, consensus or compromise as the default modus operandi. These are nongenerative patterns that run our rigid institutional hierarchies. They obstruct great flows of creativity and innovative potential. The logic of holonic systems can unleash entirely new and generative forms of human relationships and organizations in which the total is greater than the sum of the parts.

A promising alternative is *holacracy*. (See holacracy.org for more details.) The term is meant to emphasize a departure from conventional representative democracy as a governance system ("of the people, by the people and for the people") and instead embrace governance of the organization, through the people, for the *purpose*. Holacracy embeds a generative mix of autonomy and cooperation in a flexible fabric of *holonic design constitutional rules*. It constitutes a new operating system for organizations that regulate the individual/group dynamics to eliminate on one side the possibility of capture via power games, and on the other side, the inherent chaos characteristic of "leaderless," decentralized organizations.

In a holacracy, all the top-down supervisory and managerial positions are essentially torn down and replaced by accountability to the self and to the "team holon" (named Circle). Roles identify the activities and services necessary to achieve organizational/group objectives. As a "holonic organizational design technology," holacracy achieves adaptive governance through regulations that foster collaboration via flexible policymaking adjustments with a focus on disempowering ego-based competition, destructive tendencies and other forms of ineffectiveness. Such outcomes are assured by spelling out personal accountability functions for each role and by hosting a democratic process that assigns Key Roles endowed with higher authority. For example, a designated "Facilitator" ensures that the constitutional rules are followed.

Every participant in a holacracy is a sensor for what is going on, and each plays a role in identifying the tensions in a timely way while taking active steps to resolve them. Effectiveness and resistance to capture are achieved by enhancing the power of collective decision locally via procedures such as: "After taking Individual Action, a Partner should tell any affected Role about it, and, on their request, initiate actions to resolve any Tension created by the Individual Action or refrain from taking this Individual Action again in the future."

Self-organization and flexibility are ensured via policies such as: "A Circle can remove a Sub-Circle through governance by (a) removing the Sub-Circle entirely, including all Roles within it, (b) collapsing the Sub-Circle into a single Role, thus removing all Roles within it, or (c) dissolving the Sub-Circle's boundary, so that all Roles within it are absorbed by the Circle." The only valid "Governance" acts of a Circle are to create or amend Roles, Policies or Sub-Circles, or to hold elections. For a proposed Governance change to be processed and accepted, it must meet some criteria: A Proposal is generally valid for processing only if it helps one of the *Proposer's* roles, unless the Proposer has permission to process tensions for another Role. However, evolving the Governance to better reflect what's already happening is always allowed, even if unrelated to the Proposer's roles, as is calling for an election.

As a mode of governance for *purposeful organization*, holacracy works by a generative distributed authority structure designed to always sense tensions with clarity and to resolve them promptly through governance meetings. This results in healthy communion that drives group integration and "team spirit." In tactical meetings, this process results in clarifying individual accountability as it affects synchronization. As a governance system based on the rules of holonic interdependence, holacracy optimizes creative flows through a flexible organizational structure that radically changes how decisions are made and how power is distributed.

Holonic Software:
Infrastructures for Open Networks as Catalysts for Change

Since networked computing and the Internet stand at the center of societal transformation right now, it is worth asking how software design might be used to advance holonic principles. Holonics opens the perspective of designing participatory software platforms for catalyzing social networks that help people step out of hierarchies and avoid pathological organizations. Holonic-based platforms can be a tool for people to reshape society and the world by cultivating harmonious, enlivening relationships with natural ecosystems through better managing the commons. To harness the power of large-scale social ecosystems, one can conceptualize their social dynamics using holonic logic and embed holonic design rules in the network protocols and software coordinating their interactions.[11] (See Fig. 4.)

Holonics-based software can also be used to design smart infrastructures for self-stabilizing energy grids, self-deploying emergency task forces and self-reconfiguring manufacturing plants that all rely on a myriad of mobile devices, software agents and human users who use local rules and peer-to-peer communication to build their own resilient "governance" (workflow coordination) network.[12]

An intrinsic challenge in such holarchies is the "cohabitation" or integration of two ontological levels: the physical one (humans and artifacts cooperating) and the logical one (software). The logical/software ontology must emulate the physical ontology through software entities (agents) that enable the coordination of cooperative tasks. (See Fig. 4.)

This enables the deployment of a living, self-directed "digital ecology" in which humans are not just "consumers" of data and computing applications. Actors in this social network operating environment are much more: They are producers, "players" and "inputs" in a new "socio-technical combinatorics" ecosystem. Their interactions, mediated by digitally animated artifacts (mobile phones, tablets, laptops, and Google Glass-like devices and more futuristic brain implants), can be coordinated and synergistically orchestrated to steer complex, interdependent global scale systems.

Thus holonics offers a powerful "design toolbox" of methods and techniques with which to construct the architecture of such digital ecologies. Holonics can be the basis for a host of "smart infrastructures" for a sustainable world that include production, agriculture, defense, finance and the economy as a whole. In this sense, holonic institutions aspire to invent new notions of sovereignty beyond the nation-state. Yet the most important new vector of holonic sovereignty is surely the sovereignty of individual humans to protect fundamental human rights and self-organize new types of collective institutions in transnational ways.[13]

Professor Mihaela Ulieru works with many governments and organizations seeking to make ICT an integral component of policy making for a healthier, safer, more sustainable and innovation-driven world. She founded two research labs leading several large-scale projects which tackle the management of complex situations through more organic ways of governance, such as IT Revolutions, Industrial Informatics, Future of Medicine, Socio-Technical Combinatorics, Adaptive Risk Management, Living Technologies and Emulating the Mind. For her scholarship on holonics applied to mitigate global challenges in an interdependent world she was awarded, among many others, the "Industrial Research Chair in Intelligent Systems" and the "Canada Research Chair in e-Society" to explore organizational and societal transformation in the digital economy and the emergence of participatory platforms.

Notes

[1] Watts, D., *Everything is Obvious: How Common Sense Fails Us* (Random House, 2011).

[2] Bejan, A., *Design in Nature: How the Constructal Law Governs Evolution in Biology, Physics, Technology, and Social Organization* (Random House, 2012).

[3] Mella, P., *The Holonic Revolution* (Pavia University Press, 2009), available at: http://www.paviauniversitypress.it/scientifica/download/Mella-sito_2010-01-23.pdf.

[4] Mihaela Ulieru, "Adaptive Information Infrastructures for the e-Society," in *Engineering Self-Organizing Applications*, Giovanna DiMarzo Serugendo and Anthony Karageorgios (Eds.) (Berlin: Springer Verlag, 2005).

[5] Mihaela Ulieru and John Verdon, "IT Revolutions in the Industry: From the Command Economy to the eNetworked Industrial Ecosystem," Proceedings of the 1st International Workshop on Industrial Ecosystems, IEEE International Conference on Industrial Informatics, Daejoen, Korea, July 13-17 2008.

[6] Goddard, G., *Holonic Logic and the Dialectic of Consciousness*, available at http://www.integralworld.net/goddard2.html.

[7] Mella, P., *The Holonic Revolution* (Pavia University Press, 2009), available at: http://www.paviauniversitypress.it/scientifica/download/Mella-sito_2010-01-23.pdf.

[8] Geoff Mulgan, *The Locust and the Bee* (Princeton University Press, 2013).

[9] Mihaela Ulieru and Rene Doursat, "Emergent Engineering: A Radical Paradigm Shift," *International Journal of Autonomous and Adaptive Communication Systems* (IJAACS), 4(1) (2011).

[10] Don Tapscott, Global Solutions Networks, at http://gsnetworks.org.

[11] Mihaela Ulieru, "Adaptive Information Infrastructures for the e-Society," in *Engineering Self-Organizing Applications*, Giovanna DiMarzo Serugendo and Anthony Karageorgios (Eds.) (Berlin: Springer Verlag, 2005).

[12] Ibid.

[13] Don Tapscott, Global Solutions Networks, at http://gsnetworks.org.

Chapter 12

The Algorithmic Governance Of Common-Pool Resources

By Jeremy Pitt and Ada Diaconescu

Introduction: Resource Allocation in Open Systems

Using a methodology called sociologically inspired computing,[1] researchers are now attempting to solve engineering problems by developing "formal models of social processes." This entails examining how people behave in similar situations and, informed by a theory of that behavior grounded in the social sciences, developing a formal characterization of the social behavior (based on the theory) using mathematical and/or computational logic. This logical specification then provides the basis for the specification of an algorithmic framework for solving the original problem.

In networks that function as open systems, for example, a significant challenge is how to allocate scarce resources.

This is a vexing challenge because open computing systems and networks are formed on the fly, by mutual agreement, and therefore they may encounter situations at run-time that were not anticipated at design-time. Specific examples include ad hoc networks, sensor networks, opportunistic and vehicular networks, and cloud and grid computing. All these applications have at least one feature in common: the system components (henceforth referred to as *agents*) must somehow devise a means to collectivize their computing resources (processor time, battery power, memory, etc.) in a common pool, which they can then draw upon in order to achieve their individual goals in a group (or as a group) that they would be unable to do if they each functioned in isolation.

However, open systems face serious challenges in coordinating agents because there is no centralized controller-agent that is compelling other agents in the system to behave in a certain way with regards to the provision and appropriation of resources. Furthermore, all agents may be competing for a larger share of the common pool, and may therefore not comply with the requirements for "correct" (pro-social) behavior. For example, they may appropriate resources that they were not allocated, or they may appropriate resources correctly but fail to contribute expected resources (a phenomenon known as "free riding").

The Tragedy of the Commons

So, applying the first step in the methodology of sociologically inspired computing, the question is: How do people collectively allocate shared common-pool resources when there is no centralized controller "dictating" what the allocation should be? This prompts two further questions: 1) How do they solve problems such as free riding and other examples of anti-social behavior? 2) How do people allocate common-pool resources in a way that is considered *fair* by the individuals involved (in some sense of the word "fair"), and is *sustainable in the long-term* (i.e., the self-renewing resource, like a forest or fishery, is properly managed and maintained so that it is not over-used)?

One analysis of this problem, called the *tragedy of the commons,* suggests that there is *no* internal solution to this problem. According to biologist Garrett Hardin, people will inevitably deplete (exhaust) common-pool resources in the short term even if that is in no one's interest in the long-term. Many people assume that the only way to ensure that such resources are maintained is through externalized oversight by some centralized body (e.g., government) or through privatization. These solutions are not, of course, available to engineers of open computing systems.

Ostrom's Self-Governing Institutions

Although some economists believe that people will inevitably deplete common-pool resources to which they have access, the empirical data of hundreds of case studies suggests that other outcomes are possible. For example, based on extensive fieldwork, from water irrigation systems in Spain to alpine meadows in Switzerland and forests in Japan, economist and political scientist Elinor Ostrom observed that actually people tend to co-operate in such collective action situations, not only to avoid depleting the resource, but to actively maintain it, even over the course of generations.[2] Ostrom was awarded the Nobel Prize for Economic Science in 2009 for her extensive fieldwork and theoretical innovation in demonstrating the feasibility of managing common-pool resources.

The essence of the many counter-examples is this: it turns out that people are very good at *making stuff up*. In particular, people are very good at making up rules to deal with novel circumstances and challenges. Without the ability to make up rules, there would be no playing of games, for example; nor would people be able to improvise coordinated responses to emergencies. Similarly, Ostrom observed in many collective action situations, people make up rules to *self*-determine a fair and sustainable resource allocation. People voluntarily agree to abide by and regulate their behavior. Notably, these are not immutable physical laws; they are social conventions that people can and sometimes do break – either by accident, necessity or (sadly) sheer malice.

The invention of conventional rules (and their rationalization and stabilization into what Ostrom called *institutions*) is a necessary condition for preserving resources over time, but it is not a sufficient condition. On some occasions when communities develop an institution to manage their affairs, the resource is successfully sustained, but sometimes it is not. Addressing the requirement to *supply* self-governing institutions for enduring common-pool resource management, Ostrom proposed eight institutional design principles:

Boundaries: who is and is not a member of the institutions should be clearly defined – along with the resources that are being allocated;

Congruence: the rules should be congruent with the prevailing local environments (including the profile of the members themselves);

Participation: those individuals who are affected by the collective choice arrangements should participate in formulating and adopting them;

Monitoring: compliance with the rules should be monitored by the members themselves, or by agencies appointed by them;

Proportionality: graduated sanctions should ensure that punishment for non-compliance is proportional to the seriousness of the transgression;

Conflicts: the institution should provide fast, efficient and effective recourse to conflict resolution and conflict prevention mechanisms;

Autonomy: whatever rules the members agree to govern their affairs, no external authority can overrule them;

System of systems: multiple layers of provisioning and governance should be nested within larger systems.

A metareview has confirmed these principles with only minor adjustments.[3]

A Formal Characterization of Electronic Institutions

Elinor Ostrom's research provides a theory of how people can solve the collective-action problem of common-pool resource allocation. To use this theory as a basis for engineering solutions in open computing systems, three related questions must be addressed: 1) Can the theory of self-governing institutions be given a formal characterization in computational logic? 2) Can the computational logic specification be given an algorithmic interpretation that can be used to implement a self-organizing *electronic* institution? 3) Can the agents in a self-organizing electronic institution be designed according to Ostrom's eight principles so as to successfully manage and sustain a common-pool resource?

Pitt, Schaumeier and Artikis give a positive answer to all three questions.[4] The first six of Ostrom's principles were each axiomatized in first-order logic using the Event Calculus, a language used in Artificial Intelligence to represent and reason about actions and the effects of actions. This axiomatic specification was then converted into Prolog and queried as a logic program: i.e. *the specification is its own implementation*. As such, the set of clauses comprising the logic program constitutes an algorithmic specification for self-governance. Finally, the implementation was tested in a multi-agent resource allocation system that allowed clauses for each principle to be individually included in successively more complex experiments. The results showed that the more principles that were included, the more the agents (as members of the institution) were able to sustain the resource and maintain a high membership.

But Is It Fair?
Distributive Justice and the Canon of Legitimate Claims
These experiments demonstrated that Ostrom's institutional design principles for managing enduring common-pool resources could provide the basis for achieving sustainable resource allocation in open computing systems. One complication, however, is that certain elements of human social systems cannot necessarily be represented in the logic of electronic "social" systems. For example, in establishing the congruence of the provision and appropriation rules to the prevailing state of the environment (Principle 2), a software designer might assume that if Principle 3, requiring user participation in making rules, were in place, then those affected by the rules would select rules that were intrinsically or implicitly "fair." This assumption cannot be made in electronic networks whose components are without any understanding of a concept of "fairness," however.

To address this issue, Pitt, Busquets and MacBeth[5] suggest applying the methodology to another theory from the social sciences, the theory of distributive justice articulated by the philosopher Nicholas Rescher.[6] Rescher observed that distributive justice had been held, by various sources, to consist of treating people wholly or primarily according to one of seven canons (established principles expressed in English). These canons consist of equality, need, ability, effort, productivity, social utility and supply-and-demand. However, these canons each have different properties and qualities, and they therefore speak to many different (and possibly inconsistent) notions of utility, fairness, equity, proportionality, envy-free conviviality, efficiency, timeliness, etc.

Rescher's analysis showed that each canon, taken in isolation, was inadequate as the sole criterion of distributive justice. He proposed instead that distributive justice could be represented by the *canon of claims*, which consists of treating people according to their legitimate claims, both positive and negative. Then the issue of "Which is the preferred canon of distributive justice?" can be displaced by questions such as: "What are the legitimate claims in a specific context, for fairness? How can plurality be accommodated? How can conflicts be reconciled?"

Pitt, Busquets and MacBeth implemented another multi-agent system testbed and conducted another set of experiments to explore resource allocation in an economy of scarcity. (This scenario is defined as one in which there are insufficient resources at any time-point for everyone to have what they demand, but there are sufficient resources over a succession of time-points for everyone to get enough to be 'satisfied'). In this testbed, each of the canons (if it was relevant in this context) was represented as a function that computed an ordering of the agents requesting resources. To address the plurality of claims, the functions were then used in a weighted Borda Count – a voting protocol that computes an overall rank order and is more likely to produce a consensus outcome rather than a simple majoritarian outcome. To reconcile conflicts among claims, the agents themselves decided the weight to be associated with each canon in prioritizing the agents' claims.

The results showed that a group of agents, in an electronic institution based on Ostrom's principles, could self-organize a distribution of resources using the canon of legitimate claims such that it was *fair over time*. That is, while at any one time-point the resource allocation might be very unfair (using a well-known and often-used fairness metric, the Gini index), a group could nonetheless achieve allocations that were very fair over a series of time-points. The distribution could also be made fairer than alternative allocation schemes based on random assignment, rationing or strict queuing.

Socio-Technical Systems

The formalization and implementation of social processes, such as Ostrom's institutional design principles and Rescher's theory of distributive justice, provide an algorithmic basis for governance of common-pool resources in electronic social systems. These are not models of how human social systems work – but nor are they intended to be. Instead of asking if these are testable models with predictive or explanatory capacity (adequacy criteria for this are included in the methodology set forth by Jones, Artikis and Pitt[7]), a more pertinent followup question is: Can this formal approach to algorithmic self-governance be injected into open *socio-technical* systems – i.e., systems in which human participants interact with an electronically saturated infrastructure, or with each other through an electronically-mediated interface, in trying to exploit, and sustain, a common pool resource?

Here are three examples in which algorithmic self-governance could be usefully applied in socio-technical systems: decentralized community energy systems, consensus formation in open plan offices, and 'fair' information practices in participatory sensing applications.

1. In a *decentralized community energy system*, a group of geographically co-located residences may be both producers and consumers of energy. For example, the residence may have installed photovoltaic cells, small wind turbines or other renewable energy source; and the residence occupants have the usual requirements to operate their appliances. Instead of each residence generating and using its own energy, and each suffering the consequences of over- or under-production, the vicissitudes of variable supply and demand could be evened out by providing energy to a common-pool and computing a distribution of energy using algorithmic self-governance. Furthermore, excessive demand, which would otherwise lead to a power outage,

could be pre-empted by synchronized collective action in reducing consumption.

2. Similarly, *an open plan office* is a working environment that requires people to share a common space. However, a violation of conventional rules determining what is (and is not) acceptable behavior can cause instances of incivility which, if untreated, can lead to problems of escalating retaliation, a demoralized or demotivated workforce, staff turnover, and other problems. We have developed a prototype system in which we regard the (intangible) "office ambience" as a pooled resource which the office occupants can deplete by anti-social behavior and re-provision by pro-social behavior. The system interface supports consensus formation by enabling the office-workers themselves to determine what is (and is not) anti-social behavior, and supports them in detecting violations, issuing apologies and encouraging forgiveness. This is an instantiation of Ostrom's third principle – that those affected by collective choice arrangements should participate in their selection. Ostrom's fifth and sixth principles – dealing with the system of conflict prevention and resolution – should encourage pro-social behavior.

3. *Participatory sensing applications* are innovative systems that aggregate and manipulate user-generated data to provide a service. A typical example is taking users' mobile phone location and acceleration data to infer traffic density and so provide a transportation advice service. However, in many of these applications, the generators of the data are not the primary beneficiaries, and furthermore, there are severe privacy concerns over who has access to this data, how long it is stored, and what is used for. An alternative approach is to regard this user-generated data as a *knowledge commons*, and regulate access through self-determined rules, and so achieve a "fair" return of service for user-generated data.

Adaptive Institutions and Algorithmic Governance: The Way Forward

Studies in technology and law have often referred to the *law lag,* in which existing legal provisions are inadequate to deal with a social, cultural or commercial context created by rapid advances in information and communication technology (ICT).[8]

We can reasonably refer to a similar phenomenon of "institution lag," whereby the rate of technological advance far outstrips the ability of traditional institutions to adapt fast enough to track the activity it was intended to regulate. Yet adaptive institutions have been identified as a critical tool in addressing environmental challenges such as climate change and sustainability.[9]

The challenge of devising effective algorithmic governance has a lot to do with scale. We can observe that, at the micro-level, human participants are able to self-organize and self-adapt by playing various roles, but at the macro-level, the emergent outcomes of unrestricted self-organization may be ineffective or undesirable (e.g., it may result in a tragedy of the commons).

We believe that more desirable macro-outcomes may be achieved by introducing a meso-level of governance: a rule-based, ICT-enabled algorithmic framework for self-governance that is designed to assure that whatever emerges at the macro-level represents the self-identified best interests of the community's majority. The ultimate result would be to create more flexible institutions that could adapt more quickly to rapid societal changes. Since such rapid societal changes are being *caused* by ICT, it makes sense that the rapid adaptation required may be best *enabled* by ICT. Indeed, this may be the only feasible approach.

The ICT-enabled framework would provide an interaction medium that inherently implements Ostrom's rules, enabling participants to self-organize into "fair" institutions (avoiding the *tragedy of the commons*) and to self-adapt such institutions to contextual changes (avoiding the *institution lag*). Such ICT framework should enable participants to perform critical activities, such as defining community rules for resource sharing, boundary definitions and non-compliance sanctions. It should also provide core automatic functions that facilitate the participant's tasks, including for instance: managing membership based on boundary definitions; evaluating participant compliance with rules and applying sanctions; ensuring protection from external intrusion and interference; and provisioning comprehensible feedback on emerging results such as "fairness," at both micro and macro levels, which is critical for efficient rule adaptation. Finally, such a system must ensure essential properties such as overall stability, robustness and resilience, while preserving crucial social concepts like privacy, safety and security.

In this context, the meso-layer ICT framework is vital in helping to deliver the desired outcomes. This is why a platform like Open Mustard Seed (see Chapter 13), which offers designers at least the opportunity to strike the right balance between continuity and stability on the one hand, and adaptivity and responsiveness on the other, is crucial if algorithmic governance of common-pool resources, and other forms of collective action, are to be successful.

At this stage, of course, there is much that we do not know. For instance, the ICT system's *scalability* is an important concern. Here, scale relates to the total number of participants; the level of heterogeneity in targeted environments and participant profiles; the number of societal interests considered and perhaps also their cultural backgrounds; and, the incidence of conflicts among intersecting heterogeneous groups. Achieving and maintaining macro-objectives in a large-scale system composed of autonomous self-adaptive agents and situated in a continuously changing environment, will require a trans-disciplinary investigation across the social and computational sciences.

A common feature observable in most (or all?) natural systems of similar scales and dynamics, such as living organisms, societies or economies, is their reliance on *holonic* organizations (see Chapter 11 "Organic Governance Through the Logic of Holonic Systems," by Mihaela Ulieru). As first described by Arthur Koestler in the 1960s, each system element is both an autonomous entity pursuing its own objectives and controlling its internal resources as well as an element nested within a higher-level organization and contributing to its higher-level objectives by following its control commands. Recursively composing elements in this manner results in a holonic organization, or "holarchy" – a hierarchy in which each element is both autonomous yet contained within higher-level structures.

A holarchy seems essential for managing scalability issues because the structure enables problems to be detected and dealt with in isolation, at the lowest possible level, without disrupting the larger system. The holonic structure also ensures that both micro (individual) and macro (community) objectives are met concomitantly.

Successfully delivering such systems would directly satisfy Ostrom's eighth principle, i.e., a self-governing system of systems. But one of the critical difficulties here is the implementation of each community's "dual nature" as both an autonomous community with its own objectives and fairness rules and as a participant in a larger community with higher-level objectives and equity goals. This dualism reflects the built-in tensions of any individual, who naturally pursues personal objectives (selfish nature) while respecting larger community objectives (societal or transcendental nature).

Unresolved Issues

There are a number of issues that remain unresolved in devising systems of algorithmic self-governance, however. One involves the various conflicts that may occur when members belong to several communities with incompatible notions of fairness. Once these challenges are addressed theoretically, the ICT framework could in principle implement the necessary infrastructure and mechanisms for ensuring that the targeted system could self-organize into a holonic structure featuring the desired properties.

The "social ergonomics" of self-governance platforms is another important aspect that will need to be evaluated and refined. Notably, even if the macro-objectives emerging at any one time are fair with respect to a society's common good, and even if fairness is ensured in the long-term for each individual, this will not necessarily imply an acceptable *experience* for each individual in that society. For instance, while *change* may be essential for ensuring fairness in a dynamic environment, change may also cause considerable distress and discomfort to individuals experiencing it. From an individual's perspective, a relatively "unfair" state of affairs, in which they can comfortably survive in more or less stable circumstances, may be preferable to an "absolute fairness" that entails frequent and potentially dramatic changes, such as sudden progressions and regressions in their living standard. In other words, a world that is experienced as volatile may be less desirable than a certain degree of unfairness.

Yet, having algorithmic controls at their fingertips, individuals participating in a group may feel that they have no choice but to engage in a process of continuous negotiation and adaptation to rule-sets and social norms. The system's affordances would engender an open cycle of societal self-adaptations and frequent change, inducing societal stress and fatigue. Nonetheless, since *efficiency* (i.e., speed) is a defining characteristic of ICT systems, an ICT-based solution could end up introducing additional and potentially thornier problems.

There are other important questions to address:

- How vulnerable would such ICT system be to "hijacking" by external parties and what could be the consequences?
- When is fairness preferable to a certain degree of competition and could the system be re-configured to support either approach?
- Is the majority's opinion always in the community's best interest?
- Are there any collateral *costs* that such system would place on society?

Conclusions

Such questions and the ensuing design requirements must be carefully considered before irreversibly embedding societal governance in algorithmic technical systems. Since all possible scenarios cannot be predicted and addressed in advance, the ICT system itself must be sufficiently flexible to enable its evolution in parallel to the society it serves. If we can address such challenges, the potential rewards in empowering grassroots solutions to local issues (e.g., quality of experience in one's living space) and coordinating collective action on a planetary scale (e.g., ensuring resource sustainability), are incalculable. But even then, given the dismal, unresponsive performance of the alternatives to algorithmic governance and self-organization, one could even simply ask: Can we afford not to?

Jeremy Pitt is a Reader in Intelligent Systems in the Department of Electrical & Electronic Engineering at Imperial College London, UK. His research interests are in self-organizing multi-agent systems and their application to computational sustainability. He has collaborated widely, having worked on over 30 national and international projects, and has been involved in much inter-disciplinary research, having worked with lawyers, philosophers, psychologists, physiologists and fashion designers. He also has a strong interest in the social implications of technology, and had edited two volumes in this concern: This Pervasive Day *(IC Press: 2012) and* The Computer After Me *(IC Press: 2014).*

Ada Diaconescu is an assistant professor in the Computing and Networks department of Telecom ParisTech, in Paris, France. She is also a member of the CNRS LTCI research laboratory (Information Processing and Communication Laboratory). Her research interests include autonomic and organic computing, software engineering for self-adaptive and self-organising systems, component and service-oriented architectures, and interdisciplinary solutions for managing the complexity of cyber-physical systems. She received her PhD in computer science and electronic engineering from Dublin City University in 2006. Before joining Telecom ParisTech in 2009, she carried out various research projects at University of Grenoble, Orange Labs and INRIA Rhone Alpes.

Notes

[1] Andrew Jones, Alexander Artikis and Jeremy Pitt, "The Design of Intelligent Socio-Technical Systems," *Artificial Intelligence Review* 39(1):5-20, 2013.

[2] Elinor Ostrom, *Governing the Commons: The Evolution of Institutions for Collective Action*, Cambridge University Press, 1990.

[3] Michael Cox, Gwen Arnold and Sergio Villamayor Tomás, "A Review of Design Principles for Community-based Natural Resource Management," *Ecology and Society* 15(4):1-38, 2010.

[4] Jeremy Pitt, Julia Schaumeier, Alexander Artikis, "Axiomatization of Socio-Economic Principles for Self-Organizing Institutions: Concepts, Experiments and Challenges. *Trans. Auton. Adapt. Sys.* 7(4):1-39, 2012.

[5] Jeremy Pitt, Didac Busquets and Sam Macbeth, "Self-Organizing Common-Pool Resource Allocation and Principles of Distributive Justice," *submitted* to *Trans. Auton. Adapt. Sys.* (forthcoming), 2014.

[6] Nicholas Rescher, *Distributive Justice* (Bobbs-Merrill Publishing, 1966).

[7] Andrew Jones, Alexander Artikis and Jeremy Pitt, "The Design of Intelligent Socio-Technical Systems," *Artificial Intelligence Review* 39(1):5-20, 2013.

[8] Lyria Bennett Moses, "Recurring Dilemmas: The Law's Race to Keep Up with Technological Change," *Journal of Law, Technology and Privacy*, 2007(2):239-285, 2007.

[9] Royal Commission on Environmental Protection (Chairman: John Lawton). *28th Report: Adapting Institutions to Climate Change*. The Stationery Office Limited, 2010.

Chapter 13

The ID3 Open Mustard Seed Platform

By Thomas Hardjono, Patrick Deegan and John H. Clippinger

OPEN MUSTARD SEED (OMS), A PROJECT of ID3 (the Institute for Institutional Innovation by Data-Driven Design) and the M.I.T. Media Lab, seeks to develop new social ecosystems consisting of trusted self-healing digital institutions operating on open networks. The centerpiece of OMS is an open data platform that enables people to share all their personal data within a legally constituted "trust framework." This framework allows people to initiate their own "personal data store" (PDS) that can securely store and process static and dynamic data about themselves. All elements of the trust framework – open authentication, storage, discovery, payment, auditing, market making and monetized "app store" services – are based on "privacy by design" principles.

That is, privacy, security and trusted exchange are built into the very design of the system.

It is important to make these principles a functional reality in digital networks if we are going to unlock the great stores of latent value that open networks hold. As postulated by Reed's Law, the value in a network increases exponentially as interactions move from a "broadcasting model" that offers "best content" (in which value is described by the number of consumers N) to a network of "peer-to-peer transactions" (where the network's value is based on "most members," mathematically denoted as N^2). However, by far the most valuable networks are based on those that *facilitate group affiliations*. When users have tools for "free and responsible association for common purposes" the value of the network soars exponentially to 2^N.[1] (For more, see Chapter 3, "The Next Great Internet Disruption: Authority and Governance," by David Bollier and John H. Clippinger.)

The latent value of "Group Forming Networks," or GFNs, as David Reed calls them, cannot be accessed, however, unless there is an appropriate network architecture and tools. We need a network architecture and software systems that can facilitate the formation of trust and social capital in user-centric and scalable ways. This is particularly important as more sectors of commerce, governance and social life are shaped by large databases of personal information whose opaque uses are causing legitimate concerns about data security, personal privacy and social trust.

OMS is intended as a corrective. It seeks to let individuals negotiate their own social contracts regarding the uses of their personal information. By providing a consent-based platform to manage data directly and responsively, OMS enables the emergence of new sorts of effective, quasi-autonomous governance and self-provisioning. And it achieves these goals without necessarily or directly requiring government. Online communities working in well-designed software environments can act more rapidly, and with greater legitimacy than conventional government institutions.

Data Commons and Digital Law

This scenario is inspired not just by Reed's analysis of how to reap value from networks, but by the extensive scholarship of Elinor Ostrom, the Nobel Laureate in economics in 2009. Ostrom's pioneering work identified key principles by which self-organized groups can manage common-pool resources in fair and sustainable ways.[2] If data were to be regarded as a common-pool resource, Ostrom's research suggests that it would be possible for online groups to devise their own data commons to manage their personal data in their own interests. (For more on the actual design of such a platform, see Chapter 12, Jeremy Pitt and Ada Diaconescu, "The Algorithmic Governance of Common-Pool Resources.")

These insights open the possibility for the data commons to be the basis for self-organizing digital institutions in which law would have a very different character from the kinds of law we know today. The development of "digital law" in self-organizing digital institutions would enable users to devise new types of legal contracts that are computationally expressible and executable. As Bollier and Clippinger have argued, new forms of law based on computable code could provide powerful new platforms for governance and new checks against corruption and insider collusion.[3] Law could become more dynamic, evolvable and outcome-oriented, and the art of governance could be subject to the iterative innovations of Moore's Law. Designs could be experimentally tested, evaluated by actual outcomes, and made into better iterations.

A reliable system of digital law would provide an important foundation for unlocking the enormous value contained in "Big Data." One of the most robust segments of tech innovation is focused on identifying behavioral and consumer patterns in billions of telephone call records, credit card transactions, GPS location fixes and other sources as a way to learn more about consumer behavior and to make new markets. Such data also has enormous potential in improving public policies, government programs, healthcare and many other activities because they allow us to precisely measure actual behaviors and patterns of interaction among people.

This vision of a data-driven society is not likely to progress, however, unless we can develop credible systems of law and governance to protect the security and private of personal data. Open Mustard Seed seeks to provide just such a platform. The remainder of this chapter is a semi-technical discussion of the design of the OMS infrastructure. The basic goal is to let people build their own highly distributed social ecosystems for reliably governing shared resources, including access to personal data. The OMS can be viewed as a new kind of "social stack" of protocols consisting of software and legal trust frameworks for self-organized digital institutions.

The Design of Open Mustard Seed

There are two key building blocks in the architecture of OMS: the *Trusted Compute Cell* (TCC) and the *Trusted Compute Framework* (TCF).

The Trusted Compute Cell can be considered a cell unit that individuals control in order to specify and implement their personal data preferences in networked computing. A TCC can be replicated, conjoined with other cells and enhanced with capabilities that are context-specific. It helps to see the TCC from the perspective of the *social functions* it seeks to provide (as a service) to its owner. When the owner of a TCC is an individual that represents himself or herself in the virtual space, the TCC acts as an identity manager, personal data manager, registry of his or her connections (to other TCCs), and an applications execution manager, among other functions.

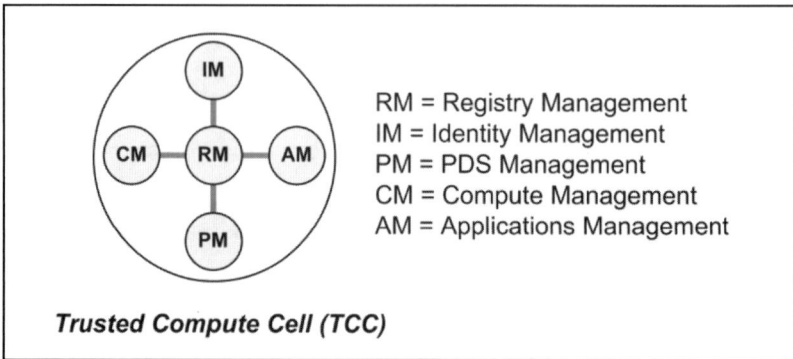

RM = Registry Management
IM = Identity Management
PM = PDS Management
CM = Compute Management
AM = Applications Management

Trusted Compute Cell (TCC)

Fig. 1: Components of the TCC

When a TCC is created to serve as an organizational unit (e.g., social group or digital institution), the TCC has the capability to provide services that pertain to groups and group-behaviors. In this case, the TCC establishes a group identity, and also performs membership management, collective data store management, shared applications management and other group-supporting services.

The OMS project designed the TCC as a cell unit from which larger digital "organisms" and social constructs can be created in network spaces. To perform these functions, the TCC must fulfill five distinct technological functions, as outlined in Fig. 2:

1. **Identity Management:** The function of identity management includes authentication, authorization, audit and log, core-identity and persona management, group identity management, assertions and claims management, single-sign-on (SSO) establishment, and others.

2. **Personal Data Store (PDS) Management:** The PDS system is a component inside the TCC that collects data (or receives streams of data) coming from the owner's devices, either generated by the device (e.g., GPS data) or proxied by the device (e.g., device pulling down copies of the owner's postings on external social network sites). The PDS system also exposes a number of APIs to external readers or consumers of the de-personalized data, such as analytics organizations and data brokers that make available the de-personalized data to the market.

   An important sub-component of the PDS system is the dynamic rule engine, which performs the role of a filtering gateway for access requests to the TCC owner's data in the PDS. The rule engine receives queries and returns answers to the querier, all the while ensuring that the responses follow the data access policies set by the owner. As such the rule engine acts as Policy Enforcement Point (PEP) for access requests to data in the PDS system.

3. **Applications Management:** Applications within the OMS architecture will be executed in the context of the calling (and managing) TCC. The owner of a TCC can stand-up an application for his or her sole use, or stand-up an application that will be shared by a group or community. A shared application can then be made accessible (to other TCCs who are community members) through its published APIs. As such, the management and instrumentation of applications is a core requirement of TCCs.

4. **Compute Power Management:** Related to applications management is the need for compute power to be expanded or reduced in an elastic manner depending on the current demand of the TCC. Elastic compute capability is particularly relevant in the case of community-shared applications, which may be shared by hundreds to millions of TCCs.

5. **Registry & Cell Management:** The registry in the TCC is the component that keeps track of identities, relationships, access policies, the TCC's memberships (to communities or institu-

tions), and others. The registry also aids in the day-to-day man-agement of the TCC by its owner. The registry acts as a Policy Administration Point (PAP) where the owner of a TCC can set policies regarding access to applications in the TCC (which is relevant in community-shared applications) and access to the owner's data in the PDS.

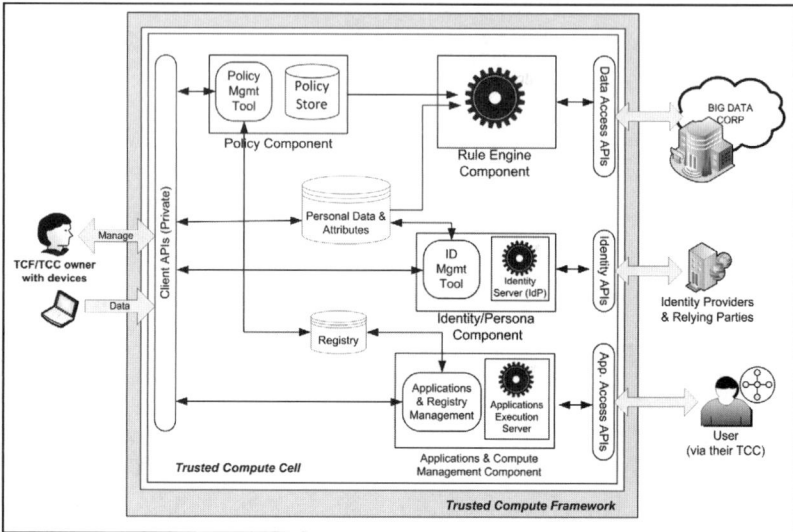

Fig. 2: Functions of the TCC

The Trusted Compute Framework (TCF)

The TCF is a larger unit of computational capability that is de-signed to operate in the virtual environment atop a virtual machine layer. One useful way to view the TCF is as a virtual resource contain-er within which one or more TCC operate. The primary purposes of the TCF are: (1) to support the secure and uninterrupted opera-tions of the TCCs; and (2) to ensure the TCF as a compute unit can operate atop the virtualization stack (e.g., hypervisor layer, security monitor layer, hardware abstraction layer, etc.) operated by the cloud provider.

Fig. 3 attempts to illustrate a generic virtualization stack with a TCF environment containing the TCCs. Fig. 3(a) illustrates a TCF with multiple TCCs, where the TCF and the TCCs are viewed as a portable constructs that are moveable from one virtualization stack to another. Fig. 3(b) shows two different TCFs (#2 and #3) running multiple TCC cells with relationships or links among them (within the same TCF and across TCFs).

Using the TCF and TCC constructs, the OMS project aims to support millions of TCCs, where each TCC represents an individual or a community. In this way the OMS platform can not only be used for peer-to-peer interactions, but also for peer-to-community and peer-to- business relationships.

The TCF is a portable compute unit which can be spun-up (and shut-down) by its owner at a TCF-compliant cloud provider (or self-operated infrastructure). The TCF is portable in that it can be relocated from one TCF-compliant cloud provider to another, using a trustworthy migration protocol.

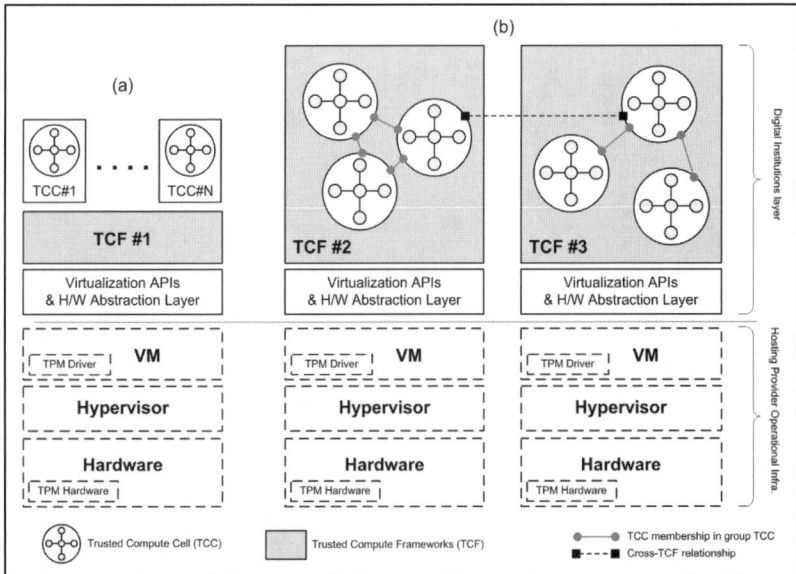

Fig. 3: The TCF and TCC

The TCF implements a number of functions to support itself as a virtual resource container:

1. **TCF administration:** As a compute unit operating atop a virtualization stack, there are administrative tasks pertaining to the operations of the TCF itself. These include secure boot-up and

shutdown under the owner's control, migration and the secure archiving of one or more TCC inside a TCF.

2. **VM provisioning & management:** When a TCF is to be launched, a virtual machine (VM) must first be provisioned that suits the desired TCF. These include processes that interact with the underlying layers (e.g., hypervisor layer), processes for memory management, processes related to security management, and others.

3. **Framework bootstrapping:** Inside the TCF, there are several processes that need to be started and managed relating to the support of the TCC. These include shared databases, API endpoints, registries, and so on. Some of these processes will be utilized by the applications that are run by the TCC.

4. **Portal, policy & applications management:** Since the TCF by design supports the importation and the running of applications as part of the TCC these applications must be instrumented and managed through the TCF. It is envisioned that much of the social network supporting applications will operate inside the TCC, allowing the TCC to support virtual individuals, groups and institutions.

5. **Security & self-protection:** As an infrastructure supporting TCCs, the TCF must provide security and resiliency against possible attacks (e.g., DDOS attacks from external sources, interference from adjacent VMs in a multitenant environment, etc.).

Security and Privacy Considerations

There are a number of security and privacy requirements for a TCF/TCC design and implementation. These features protect the user's personal data in the Personal Data Store inside the TCC, and assure that the TCF operates as a virtualized resource container in the manner for which it was designed, regardless of the cloud provider platform on which it is running. Some key security and privacy requirements include *unambiguous identification* of each TCC instance, *unhindered operations* of a TCC instance and its enveloping TCF, and *truthful attestations* reported by a TCC instance regarding its internal status.[4]

There are a number of new and emerging trustworthy computing technologies that can be used to address some of the security and privacy requirements of the TCC and TCF design. For example, a hardware-based *root of trust* could be used as the basis for truthful attestations regarding not only the TCF (and the TCCs it supports), but also for the entire virtualization stack. The wide availability of hardware such as *Trusted Platform Module* (TPM)[10] on both client and server hardwares can be used as a starting point to address the security needs of the TCF and TCC. Cloud providers that seek to provide high assurance services could make use of these technologies to increase the security of their virtualization infrastructure.[4] Features such as "trusted boot" of a TCF could be deployed more widely if these trustworthy computing hardwares were deployed by cloud providers.

A number of features of the TPM hardware could be used today to increase the security of the TCF and TCC. For example, the "sealing" capability of the TPMv2.0 hardware could be used to provide data-at-rest security to a TCF. In such a scenario, when in-rest (not in operation) a TCF could be encrypted and the keys then be bound to a given hardware platform (e.g., bound to the TPM hardware belonging to the cloud provider or the TPM hardware in the owner's portable device). In this way, the launching of the TCF can be cryptographically possible only with the presence of the TCF-owner (i.e., a human owner). Similarly, a secure "TCF migration" protocol could be envisaged based on the migration protocol designed for the TPM hardware.[5] Such a migration protocol would allow a TCF-owner to safely move their TCF from one cloud provider to another with a higher degree of assurance.[6]

How TCC and TCF Enable Users to Self-Organize OMS Communities

A key aim of the OMS project is to provide new infrastructure for the Internet that enables people to create their own highly distributed social ecosystems for governing shared resources, including their personal data. The OMS uses the notion of *manifests* to express modes of operations for a given TCF as well as the rules of behavior for a community that has been established using a TCF.

When one or more users seek to establish a self-organizing community, they must define the purpose of the community and a number of "operating rules" that are expressed internally within the TCF as manifests. Some of these operating and behavioral rules can be complex. For example, the manifest must be able to represent and implement:

- how the group is to be formed, governed, managed and evolved;
- how users interact and share information based on individual consent;
- what data is collected, and how they are accessed, stored and logged/audited;
- access policies and access-control mechanisms by which the data is protected;
- how a user may join, suspend or withdraw from the community or institution, and how their personal data can be extracted upon departure; and
- what data is retained regarding a departed user and the fact of his/her participation in the community or institution.

It is worth emphasizing here that a human person may participate in several digital communities, own and operate multiple TCFs, and thereby have "slices" of their personal data spread across several digital communities (without any sharing of information among those communities). In all these instances, OMS requires individual consent, control over personal data, and data sharing as an opt-in choice. The personal data stores are heterogeneous distributed repositories to protect the individual against unauthorized collection of data, inference and linking of data that violates the privacy of the individual.[7]

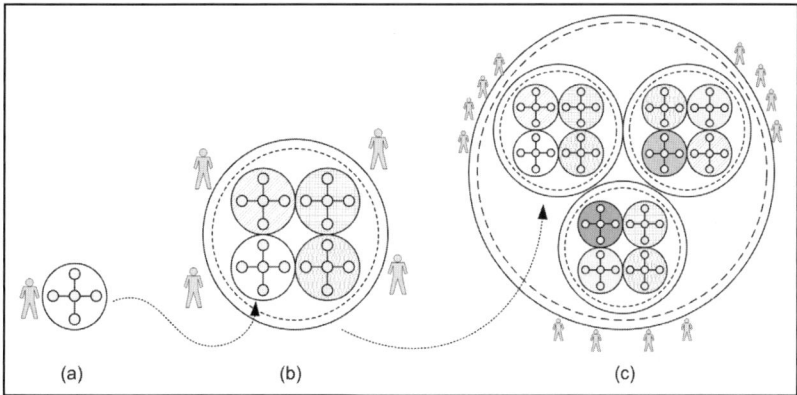

Fig. 4: Portal TCCs and Community TCCs

Private and Portal TCCs

The design of the TCC is intended to allow TCCs to be re-combinable and embeddable units of logic, computation and storage. An individual person at minimum can represent himself or herself as a solitary unit by creating a lone or private TCC cell contained within a TCF (see Fig. 4(a)).

However, life becomes more interesting for that person if he or she participates in a digital community through the use of one or more TCCs that he or she owns and controls. Using the same cell paradigm, the person can launch another distinct TCC that he or she can then use to establish a community-shared TCC. We refer to this as a Portal TCC because it represents an entry-point or portal to a shared TCC running shared applications. This is abstractly shown in Fig. 4(b).

A portal TCC allows its creator to predefine the purpose of the TCC, the applications allowed to operate in the TCC and the rules-of-operation (manifests) that govern the TCC. A complete and functioning portal TCC is thus referred to as a Community TCC. In order to be accepted into and participate within a Community-TCC (Fig. 4(b)), an individual newcomer must agree (opt-in) to the terms of participation of the community as expressed in that TCC's manifest. Such manifests are accessible through public APIs as a means for "discovery" of resources in that Community-TCC. When a Portal-TCC

(Fig. 4(b)) seeks to participate in a larger community, we refer to it as an Institution-TCC. An Institution-TCC has its own manifests that must be accepted by Community-TCCs and individual TCCs before they can join the Institution-TCC.

A New Stack for the Future Internet

In order for society to obtain the benefits of personal data as the new asset class, a new personal data ecosystem must evolve where every stakeholder has equitable access to data and other resources within the ecosystem. Such equitable access must be available not only to individuals in real-world communities, but also to emerging digital communities and institutions.

We believe that a new vision is needed for seeing the Internet, personal data and digital institutions in a consistent manner, something akin to the Internet TCP/IP stack or the 7-layer ISO stack. Such a stack – termed the digital institution stack[8] – would be useful for viewing the evolving personal data ecosystem and its role in the digital institution. Such a logical set of layers or "stack" allows the stakeholders in the ecosystem to understand better their roles in the ecosystem and to define with greater clarity the services or functions that they offer, and the services of other stakeholders upon which they rely. Fig. 5 illustrates one such possible stack.

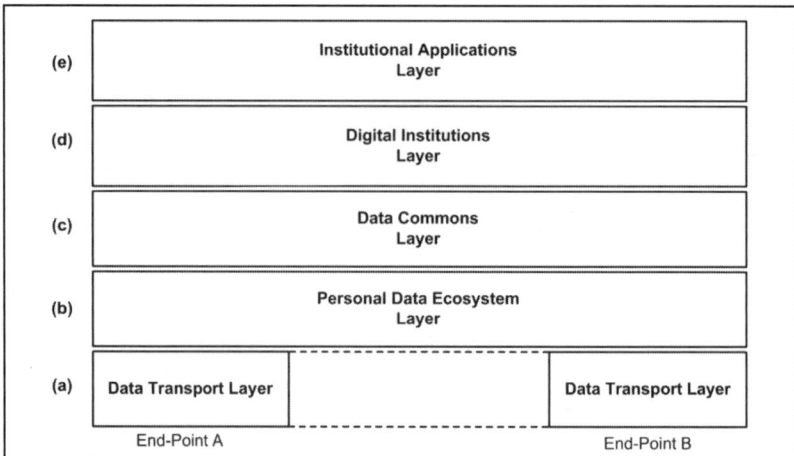

Fig. 5: A New "Digital Institutions Stack" for the Internet

The digital insitutions stack in Fig. 5 consist of the following layers (from bottom to top):

(a) *Data Transport Layer:* This is essentially the Internet as we know it today, including the various propietary social networks.

(b) *Personal Data Ecosystem Layer:* This layer contains the personal data ecosystem entities. This ecosystem is today in its nascent state, as a number of infrastructure requirements – both technical and legal infrastrctures – need to be established before individuals and organizations are willing to share their data in an equitable manner.

(c) *Data Commons layer:* This layer builds upon the layer beneath it by making data – personal data and institutional data – available to the broader population of Internet users as a common-pool resource and under a distributed legal trust framework or contract. The consumers of the data may not belong to a given community in the personal data ecosystem, but in order to access any data in the common pool they must sign on to the legal trust framework.

(d) *Digital Institutions Layer:* Certain specific "digital institutions" or communities may emerge that rely upon one or more data pools within the underlying layer. This is the 4th layer from the bottom of the stack in both Fig.s 5 and 6. The idea here is that certain online organizations or communities can be established for specific purposes that make use of the common-pool data and provide value-added to their members.

We believe cross-layer distributed legal trust frameworks will play a key role in the future. The distributed legal trust framework that governs this worldwide digital organization must not be in conflict with the frameworks that govern the pools of data from which it reads. As such, we believe there will be a growing need for *distributed legal trust frameworks*, which amount to contracts that are verifiable through computation – a version of the so called "computational law" engine.

(e) *Institutional Applications Layer*: The uppermost layer is the institutional applications layer – something akin to Layer 7 of the ISO Internet model. A digital institution may use the data, which it obtains from the layer below, for multiple applications.

Fig. 6 provides a concrete example of how this new stack of protocols could facilitate new types of scaleable, trusted uses of data. We use a hypothetical Australian vineyard, but we could just as easily illustrate the workings of this stack for data from other domains, such as data from the health science areas and cancer research. In our example, a small vineyard collects various data and puts them into its own Vineyard PDS (Personal Data Store). This data is localized to the vineyard, and some of its data points maybe context-specific to that region of Australia (e.g., land quality, temperature ranges, etc.).

As we see in Layer c, the "Data Commons Layer," the many local vineyards in Australia may wish to establish a common pool of vineyard data covering all or the majority of vineyards in Australia. Depending on the legal trust framework governing this data pool, certain identifying information could be removed (either when the data are contributed into the data pool, or when any data are read from the established data pool). Similarly, a group of European vineyards could create their own common pool of data pertaining to their members (and their members only).

But imagine that a worldwide digital organization of craft winery enthusiasts decides that it would like to access data from the Australian as well as from the European common pools of data. As shown in Layer d of Fig. 6, this fictitious digital organization could, for example, perform in-depth data analysis and make the findings available to its members. The availability of fine-grain data from the PDS of the members (two layers below) could be exposed to the organization, thus making its predictions about future yields from different regions of the world more accurate. But such fine-grain analysis would be possible only if local vineyards agreed to share their data through standards APIs to the data commons layer; if the vineyards could see commercial value of sharing the data; and if the privacy protections provided at the digital institutions layer were reliable and secure.

To take this hypothetical one step further, the fictitious digital organization (the worldwide association of craft wineries) may wish to establish a digital currency system that is asset-backed – using the very data in the common pools as the backing for the currency. The accuracy and provenance of the data in these data pools (at the personal data ecosystem layer, b, would become crucial to the viability of digital assets trading of the future.

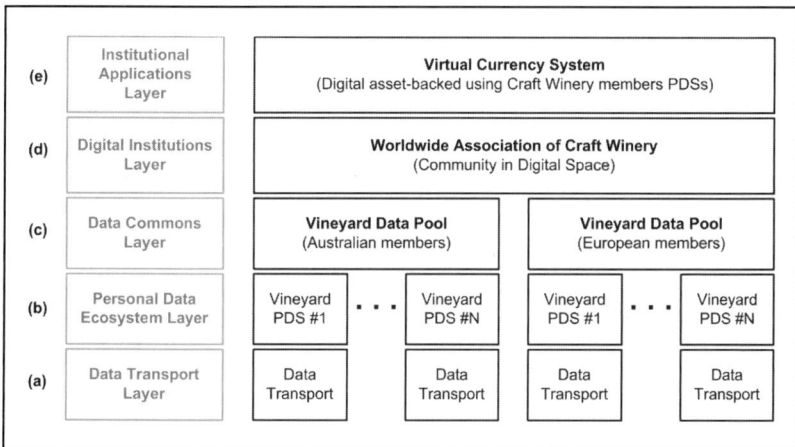

(e)	Institutional Applications Layer	Virtual Currency System (Digital asset-backed using Craft Winery members PDSs)			
(d)	Digital Institutions Layer	Worldwide Association of Craft Winery (Community in Digital Space)			
(c)	Data Commons Layer	Vineyard Data Pool (Australian members)		Vineyard Data Pool (European members)	
(b)	Personal Data Ecosystem Layer	Vineyard PDS #1 ... Vineyard PDS #N		Vineyard PDS #1 ... Vineyard PDS #N	
(a)	Data Transport Layer	Data Transport	Data Transport	Data Transport	Data Transport

Fig. 6: Example of Digital Communities and Digital Institutions

Conclusions and Future Work

There are a number of future challenges that we want to address using the OMS as a platform for research:

A new Internet stack for digital institutions: There is a need to broaden the notion of "layers" of the (future) Internet by introducing a new "stack." Such a stack should identify distinct layers pertaining to the personal data ecosystem, the open data commons, and digital institutions. Just as in the Internet stack of today, in the *Digital Institutions Stack* each layer makes use the of "services" of the layer below it, while exposing new services and APIs to the layers above it. We envision that new Internet services will appear in each of the layers, and that each layer will evolve to become an ecosystem unto itself.

Computational law: The notion of self-governance is core to the value proposition of communities operating using the TCF and TCC constructs. As such, there needs to be a new perspective regarding "law as algorithm" where rules could be automatically enforced by the TCCs. In other words, law, by common agreement, could be made self-enforcing in communities that operate the TCFs and TCCs. The rule engine inside the TCC could be developed into a digital "law enforcement engine."

Protocols for personal data exchange: A new generation of protocols needs to emerge that view Personal Data Stores (contained within TCCs) as legitimate API end-points. Such a protocol would be key to making personal data a true digital asset. Not only would these new protocols exchange data, but also observe, negotiate and enforce the legal trust frameworks governing the usage of personal data.

Thomas Hardjono *is Technical Lead and Executive Director of the M.I.T. Consortium for Kerberos and Internet Trust. Hardjono acts as a liaison with key external stakeholders who participate within M.I.T.-KIT community, and as the technical lead establishes the strategic direction of its projects.*

Patrick Deegan *is Chief Technology Officer of ID3 and Lead Architect of OMS.*

John H. Clippinger *is Executive Director and CEO of ID3 and Research Scientist at the M.I.T. Media Lab Human Dynamics Group.*

We wish to thank Professor Alex (Sandy) Pentland from the M.I.T. Media Lab for his support in this work as well as Stephen Buckley from the M.I.T. Kerberos and Internet Trust (M.I.T.-KIT) consortium for his ongoing support.

References

[1] David P. Reed, "That Sneaky Exponential – Beyond Metcalfe's Law to the Power of Community Building," 1999, available on http://www.reed.com/dpr/locus/gfn/reedslaw.html.

[2] Elinor Ostrom, "Beyond Markets and States: Polycentric Governance of Complex Economic Systems," 2009, Nobel Prize Lecture, December 8, 2009. Available on http://www.nobelprize.org.

[3] David Bollier and John Henry Clippinger, "The Next Great Internet Disruption: Authority and Governance," ID3, 2013, available on http://idcubed.org.

[4] See, e.g., Trusted Computing Group, "TPM 1.2 Specifications" (2011), available on http://www.trustedcomputinggroup.org; and J. Zic and T. Hardjono, "To-

wards a Cloud-based Integrity Measurement Service," *Journal of Cloud Computing: Advances, Systems and Applications*, (February 2013).

[5] Trusted Computing Group, "TCG Interoperability Specifications for Backup and Migration Services (v1.0)," Trusted Computing Group, TCG Issued Specifications, (June 2005), http://www.trustedcomputinggroup.org/resources.

[6] S. Berger, R. Caceres, K. A. Goldman, R. Perez, R. Sailer, and L. van Doorn, "vTPM: Virtualizing the Trusted Platform Module," in *Security 06: 15th USENIX Security Symposium* (Vancouver, Canada, July-Aug 2006), available on www.usenix.org.

[7] Alex Pentland, "Data Driven Societies," 2012, available on http://media.mit.edu/pentland. See also World Economic Forum, "Personal Data: The Emergence of a New Asset Class," 2011, available on http://www.weforum.org/reports/personal-data-emergence-new-asset-class.

[8] Thomas Hardjono, Patrick Deegan and John Henry Clippinger, "On the Design of Trustworthy Compute Frameworks for Self-Organizing Digital Institutions," in *Proceedings of the 2014 Human-Computer Interactions International Conference* (June 2014).

Chapter 14

The Relational Matrix:
The Free and Emergent Organization
of Digital Groups and Identities

By Patrick Deegan

THE INTERNET WAS INITIALLY ARCHITECTED WITHOUT consideration for a secure, viable identity infrastructure. Passwords were an afterthought and there was little consideration given to privacy and how individuals could assert control over their personal data. There have been many attempts to remedy these shortcomings and there are growing open source and industry initiatives to deal with these issues.[1] These factors combined with the move towards "personal data clouds," mobile and sensor data, and the recognized importance of protecting and sharing personal data, is forcing a fundamental rethinking of the global Internet architecture for secure and privacy-preserving communications and computations.

What is clear is that the current infrastructure cannot be simply uprooted and replaced, and that the next "authentication, privacy and sharing layer" has to grow organically on top of the existing layer. Fortunately, a combination of technologies for the self-deployment and administration of services with new encryption, identity authentication and access controls technologies and protocols are making it feasible to scale new self-deploying infrastructures. Such new approaches make it possible for social groups to naturally emerge where individuals can control their own personal data in many ways that allow for a balanced, transparent and law-based approach for expressing and enforcing individual and group data rights. The Open Mustard Seed (OMS) platform represents an open source effort to enable such an architecture on a global scale.

Background

The Open Mustard Seed project is an opensource Trust Framework for developing and deploying web apps in a secure, user-centric personal cloud.[2] In this sense, it is both a Platform as a Service model (PaaS) as well as a basis for building global digital identity infrastructure and data asset ecosystems. Specifically, a Trust Framework is a combination of software mechanisms, contracts, and rules for defining, governing, and enforcing the sharing and protection of information.

A typical Trust Framework is described and often decomposed into Technical and Operational Specifications in conjunction with a set of legally binding Rules (Policies). Thus, the system itself is designed to orchestrate and execute the specifications and policies according to common, predictable, and independently verifiable standards of performance. The goal is for all parties to trust that the system will regulate, enforce and maintain the obligations of all participants in a transparent and auditable manner. To this end, we focus on the development of an ecological model for social/civic engagement, one that provides identity assertions in a manner such that all relying parties are subject to independent and autonomous contracts for data rights enforcement, whether those participants are represented by individuals, groups (e.g., elected representatives), system entities (e.g., autonomous agents), companies or even governments. In this sense, the Open Mustard Seed Trust Framework defines the processes and procedures that provide mutual assurance between "Institutions" and Decentralized Autonomous Organizations (DAO) and Decentralized Autonomous Authorities (DAAs) with respect to privacy, performance and remediation.

One of Open Mustard Seed's main goals is to operationalize the creation of decentralized digital institutions in a generic framework, emphasizing Don't Repeat Yourself (DRY) principles. In doing so, we recognize the need for a framework that allows for interoperability at scale, while providing a development environment for applications that can specify the requirements and rules that govern user participation in an extensible and reusable manner.

Below are some of the criteria reflecting a NSTIC (National Strategy for Trusted Identities in Cyberspace) perspective on organically creating an operational and autonomous Trust Framework:[3]

- Register devices (e.g., Quantified Self, Internet of Things, Personal Robotics) and associate / manage self-enforcing policies in the Trust Networks originated by the user;

- Assign access control policies on Personal APIs with built in support for a combination of "building blocks" that constitute a Trust Framework;

- Automate digital asset custodianship in a manner that can be independently audited (e.g., demonstrate standardized policy enforcement or regulatory compliance execution for data retention, logging, provenance, metatagging, etc.) and verified-grounding trust in various algorithmically proven metrics for system-wide transparency;

- Allow the user to extend Personas (user driven data objects containing attributes, scopes and a pseudonymous digital identity) in a privacy-preserving manner to allow them to advertise any associated data rights assigned to the Persona to create an ecosystem of client networks (e.g., integrate with digital currency platforms, law enforcement, social networks, etc.) in a consistent manner for the user;

- Allow Groups to provide structure for automating system deployment as a natural, holonic network, enabling all applications built upon the framework to exploit the "centralization" of data originated at multiple interdependent scales. Groups themselves can generate valid Personas;

- Establish an evolving basis from which users can assert their personal identity. OMS requires the dialog to include the users themselves as new standards are codified and OMS is continuously improved upon;

- Participate in contractually executed compute and data aggregations, generating new APIs and verifiable chains of trust-allowing users to anchor sovereign identity and apply relations to simultaneously meet the needs of participation in a multitude of social and trust-based networks (the Groups in the digital space around them). Data rights as assigned by Personas applies to Group Personas, thus operationalizing another holonic dimension – aggregation of scopes of dynamically registered group members' clients and the DAO contractually managed linking/delinking that allows for unwrapping of members' rootID's and their respective Personas' attributes (e.g., unwrapping counterparty risk with ability to view signed and time-stamped snapshots and compare against realtime quantification) in a manner that is independent of any party or actor in the system;

- Integrate with a secure discovery service in the form of a Decentralized Autonomous Organization asserting itself as a publicly accessible Portal Trusted Compute Cell (TCC) with APIs that provide Persona lookup CoreID verification services while meeting the recommendations of the Jericho Forum "Identity Commandments";

- Contract posting maintenance to be carried out by registered pseudonymous Personas; and

- Provide a basis for humans to manage multiple digital identities and give them agency to act on their behalf, while engaging in automated processes to discover and curate the relations these Persona could form by participating in Trust Networks for the mutual benefit of the whole ecosystem having to implement the commons and use digital currency as shared resource.

Thus the Trust Framework itself provides *a stack of core technologies that work together to provide a high level of security and ease of use when computing upon sensitive information.* This includes: sharing and collecting personal and environmental data; controlling Web-enabled devices; engaging with others to aggregate information and view the results of applied computation via protected services; and participating in market creation and clearing events that allow parties to execute contracts that set forth the rules and obligations when it applies to managing and exchanging data rights and their associated risks.

The Hierarchy of Structural Decompositions in OMS

Trust Network
- Defines context, curation of institutional policies
- Containment for common norms or system-wide contractual obligations
- Utilizes Decentralized Autonomous Organization (DAO) technologies at various scales for the automated provisioning of trusted resources in conjunction with Personas and Groups

Trusted Compute Cell
- Deployable Virtual Machine; Implements core functionality, patterns
- Hosts containers, scalable computation
- Exposes RESTful APIs
- Authentication/Authorization via Policy Manager driven OpenID Connect

Trusted Application Bundle
- Application deployment pattern
- Decentralized platform integrity assurance

Open Mustard Seed Root Identity modules
- Groups
- Personas
- Root Identity Infrastructure with Biodynamic Authentication and Secure Element or Trusted Platform Module (TPM) backed rootID

Trust Network

In OMS, Trust Networks form distinct ecosystems. That is, an enterprise, an NGO, government agency, social network, academic institution, an artist collective or even an individual, can each host its own private cloud defining their own set of rules – while still remaining beholden to the organizational structures they exist within (e.g., automatic regulatory compliance based on physical location). Even though these are thought of as distinct Trust Networks, the virtual and physical infrastructure that composes them are likely to be massively varied and shared amongst many. For example, a Trust Network can be defined as the internal chat network that family members use to sync amongst themselves and thus might be contained in a small set of virtualized services hosted from a single source, such as their home entertainment system. On the other side of the spectrum, OMS could be used to develop a clone of a global social network (Facebook), only it would be distributed, autonomous and under the control of a group comprised of billions of Personas, accountable to user-centric data control, completely personalized, etc.

Noting that Trust Networks can also scale to be as complex as serving a multiplicity of simultaneous purposes, OMS employs federated single sign-on and user-managed access models to orchestrate massively distributed aggregations of data. To make managing such a deployment even feasible, any solution must embrace system design principles that emphasize stability-enhancing behavior. Thus OMS takes an ecological approach for the composition of services running at different sources with different users/admins at many levels in the hierarchy. Living systems are organized in such a way that they form multi-leveled structures, each level consisting of subsystems which are wholes in regard to their parts, and parts with respect to the larger wholes.[4] We call systems that exhibit these properties a "holarchy" and the individual units themselves are known as "holons." (See Chapter 11, "The Logic of Holonic Systems," by Mihaela Ulieru.) This enables Trust Networks in OMS to provide a middle ground between network and hierarchical structures, and exhibit four basic characteristics:

- Self-preservation
- Self-adaptation
- Self-Referencing
- Self-dissolution

Trusted Compute Cell

OMS allows developers to implement web services that are easily queued, monitored, and decommissioned in a trusted environment in the cloud. This is accomplished by use of secure computational containers. A Trusted Compute Cell (TCC) is the virtualized equivalent of the minimal Trust Network (a Group of one) that remains fully interoperable within OMS. TCCs are currently defined around industry standard Virtual Machine environments. For instance, a TCC can be deployed to the Rackspace Public Cloud (via OpenStack) or be hosted within a Public Cloud's virtualized environment (VirtualBox); both are equivalent for all intents and purposes.

Since they provide all the privileges of a DAO, TCCs are typically employed as the basic unit of individual control over their data. That is, each Trusted Compute Cell (TCC) can serve as a Persona Manager for the user, providing the necessary operations in order to issue credentials in accordance with attribute-based access control policies. In its simplest form, an online digital identity is formed by users establishing their rootID within a TCC, allowing them to authenticate and grant themselves access to their own data. High assurances can be granted to the user by establishing a verifiable hardware and software chain of trust in conjunction with biometric based authentication. Fortunately, this functionality can be automated through the manner in which the TCC is configured.

From this point, the system architecture uses nested tiers of Trusted Compute Cells networking the individual, fully controlled cell (Private TCC) with other self-governed Group TCCs, and publicly accessible Portal TCCs. The idea is to enable trusted social relationships and collaboration that can scale.

Central to the proposition that users should control their own data is the Personal Data Store (PDS). For the user, access to their PDS resource is regulated through their TCC. The TCC enforces API permissions logic, referring to the user's privacy and sharing settings to determine whether to allow a particular operation on an API. This allows TCCs to provide protected access to shared data for the purpose of computing results that do not violate the rules and permissions of users, the installed applications, or the Trust Network wherein they reside.

A user's private sphere/hub is the set of Private TCCs that oversee his or her identities and personal data services. From this perspective, the user can see all of his or her data. This root/hub presents visibility/accessibility into all that "grows" from the data (the identity anchor point from which all builds in relation to), as illustrated below:

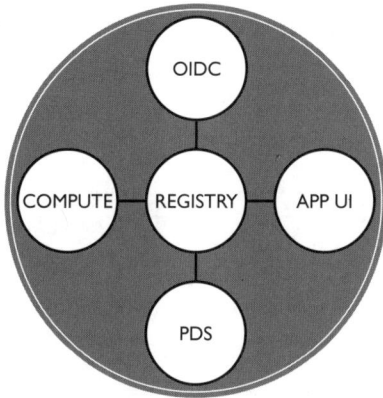

Network of Virtual Resources
under control of Registry

Personal registry for the data
- All that the user collects, produces, manages, distributes, (for which they exercise their data rights).
- Privacy settings
- Linkage to social hubs or aggregation points, interfaces to curate personas
- Dashboard for managing the installation and availability of apps and services

OMS as a trusted compute infrastructure enables users to contribute to or interact with collective computation (serving the members of trusted group as well). Although there is a significant complexity in the underlying infrastructure, OMS is designed so that the individual and even developers are shielded from this complexity by higher level interfaces that simplify both privacy setting and sharing choices and the requirements of developers to comply with privacy and security policies.

Trusted Application Bundle

The Trusted Application Bundle, or TAB, contains digital legal contracts that outline the opt-in terms of agreement for online interactions provided by the deployment of the APIs contained within the TAB's Manifests. These agreements are subsequently enforced, on behalf of the persona – within the TCF to which the TAB instance was deployed. Furthermore, TABs specify what data may be collected, accessed, stored, how it may be used, etc.; what access-control mechanisms and policies will govern data; and the "constitutional rules" by which groups may form, manage themselves, and evolve.

To a user, Groups may be logically separated by the classes of contractual obligations they opt-into upon registering a Persona within the group context (data rights grant) or by installing a TAB and inviting other personas to join that TAB's group. The installable TABs may be specified (and even distributed) by the entity hosting the Trust Framework and are the means for the institution to reflect rules and permissions options granted to its members. Thus, every Group is anchored and deployed in the context of its governing Trust Networks via association with a particular instance of an installed TAB. This is the relational matrix that reflects the meaningful information to the user.

Distributed systems can form such that each node can originate independently yet still remain interoperable across trans-institutional boundaries. Yet still, in OMS, the physical infrastructure and the software running on it determine a measurable or quantifiable Quality of Service for each distinct instance of a deployed TAB. This Interface/ Abstraction Boundary also facilitates application of existing third-party certification of protocols and standards.

It is common for users to have groups they would like to keep separate (fully secure) but still be able to make chat connections with within a single interface. This potentially requires that they maintain completely separate virtual infrastructure, including root-of-trust pathways for each instance of the client application. In order to facilitate standardization around deployment patterns, we modularize around the TAB, allowing multiple instances to be installed and associated with distinct personas. A user may also replicate their deployments across many different hosted systems for added assurances around redundancy, availability, security, etc. This enables hosting to be commoditized at every scale.

It is like having separate copies of Skype running for each alias you might use day-to-day: colleague, friend, family, etc. However, with OMS the perspective can be controlled by the user or their proxy since they are the only ones that can re-aggregate all of their personas. This enables the UX to present views that are composed from data aggregated across various sets of their persona allowing for unified, convergent visualizations, reconstructing the 360-degree view of themselves.

TABs further include provisions for enforcing:
- What data is collected, accessed, stored, logged, etc.
- How users interact and share information
- How groups are formed, governed, managed, and evolved (See Chapter 12, "The Algorithmic Governance of Common-Pool Resources," by Jeremy Pitt and Ada Diaconescu)
- How Markets and Exchanges can be built on top of decentralized data rights through contract enforcement

Identity Infrastructure

A root identity infrastructure provides a way for each person to own their single underlying root identity (i.e., the "Core Identity") and to bind several Personas to that Root Identity without the need for other parties to access the Root Identity or be aware of any other persona.

The root of the chain of trust is anchored to a single physical token. From there a user can generate many downstream Personas – in this case, for use within an infrastructure that provides "authentication as a service." This means that user-centered and user-owned Root Identities can be leveraged for a "claims-based" federated identity without giving up the Root Identity or unique information to every requesting party or other counter party or being aware of any other persona. Furthermore, it is possible for multiple aliases, accounts, and attributes to be authenticated in a reliable, privacy enhancing, and scalable manner.

In relationship to PDS or digital vault, rootID cryptographically originates keys for decrypting and controlling access to PDS. As such, rootID is portable and allows the user to backup "credentials." OMS realizes that unless there is a framework enabling interoperability, each institution could possibly offer a unique data 'vault' to their customer leading to massive fragmentation of the user's "identity."

Bootstrap rootID

Open Mustard Seed is developing a open registration and authentication algorithm for supporting sovereign identities that are bootstrapped by the user and carry attributes verified by their online interactions and by attribute authorities within the rootID infrastructure. Users can install a native app that collects data to establish a biometric/behavioral "fingerprint" (Personal data + Social Interactions + Sensor Data = Unique "Signature") for themselves to be used as their credential for authenticating into their Private Clouds.[6] The native App further provides data-driven services (via a secure vault for storing high-value personal data assets) and sets up OMS in the background. This can be done such that the user doesn't see any difference from how they install apps today except for the obvious notices about their data and opt-in agreements will be OMS.

Moreover, the Private TCC is meant to run in a myriad of locations where there is no central administrator. This ensures that when user's data is imported, provenance/origination/indexing/meta-tagging/filtering/etc. will be automatically applied, as obligated by the installed governance principles, independent of the deployment.

What is a Persona?

A persona represents an aspect of a user's digital identity. Granting a persona to an external (to the user) agent represents delegating an aspect of the user's self to that agent. A good way to think about this relationship would be as a power of attorney: a physical being authorizes some legally recognized entity to act on their behalf in some capacity. That entity is implicitly granted any access required in order to fulfill that capacity, and anything done by that entity is considered as if done by the physical being directly.

Moreover, a persona is a self-contained composite object with embedded data or attributes. These attributes contain a list of scopes that determine the access the persona can be granted for a particular API. Thus, when a persona is granted to a client, the client is implicitly granted any scopes it has in common with the persona. In order to provide a convenience to the user, Personas can be created with different sets of scopes, consistent with particular contexts of the user. For instance, a "banking" Persona can be specified with a set of scopes that enable applications to access a user's financial information while a "friends and family" Persona could provide access to a user's photos and calendar information.

Besides containing scopes as attributes, Personas can carry generic information and provide a means for user to interact with other users in a trusted manner without revealing personal information. That is, personas are either anonymous, pseudo-anonymous, partially verified or fully verified. Verified Personas have attributes that have been digitally signed by a rootID Attribute service so that services can determine the validity of claims that Personas present without requiring direct access to the user that created the Persona in the first place. [7]This data-driven functionality builds from initial provisioning of rootID. This process anchors the user's identity in digital equivalent, PDS vault containing the "body" of Personal Information the user owns/controls. Subsequently, the user projects their identity through the equivalent to "identity proxies" or Personas. This allows the user to participate in particular contexts without having their identity exposed (or personal data leaked about them without their expressed approval).[8]

OMS solves a number of interrelated problems about Big Data and the digital marketplace. A user may not know with whom they are really transacting, nor can they readily verify that their privacy preferences are actually respected and enforced. Users are often wary of exposing or sharing their data with third parties whose trustworthiness is not known. In this context, it is not surprising that protecting one's personal information is seen as antithetical to commercial and governmental uses of it. However, users can now think of creating Personas in cases where they would like to control their privacy, e.g., use a persona for making an online payment where one of the attributes is a single-use authorization code. A Vendor can access Persona Attributes to verify shipping information, buyer reputation, etc. Both parties can feel protected while subject to automated dispute resolution and other protections.

Users have not had an easy or reliable means to express their preferences for how their personal data may be accessed and used, especially when one context (a bank) differs so much from another (a healthcare provider) and still others (family and friends). As a convenience for the user, each Persona can represent a different social norm or set of preferences, from which derivatives can easily be generated. This is so the user is not overwhelmed with managing the privacy preferences separately for each context.

Instead, for each context a user creates generalized / segmentation / template Personas and reuses them. For the default cases, Personas can be defined and automatically prepopulated. Other Personas could be based on the results of predictive analytics applied to the user's behavior in such a manner that these Persona are highly likely to match the user's actual preferences, i.e., machine-learning can predict most likely preferences and auto populate a Persona and then automatically apply it to the context / application domain.

"Ideally" every user wears self-initializing hardware rootID (Secure Element) that contains specialized hardware to generate public / private keypair physically tied to the user. Since the private key never needs to leave these devices and cannot be accessed from outside, rootIDs, personas can be derived and used to represent the user in online transactions, and can all be trusted to a standard level of performance.

For the most secure and trusted systems, there needs to be rootID installed at the sensor / chip level for every device that exists within the Trust Framework. Even keyboards built into mobile devices themselves or user "owned" virtual machines would also need to be paired with a secure element – if they are intended to be interoperable with any component of a Trust Framework that required a highly available chain of trust validation service.

The more the infrastructure can provide the appropriate level of assurance automatically, for a given context, the more self-enforcing trusted transactions can become the norm. Presently a tremendous wave of new data-driven market ecologies is poised to thrive, including robotics, Internet of Things, Quantified Self, geolocal-social trends.

Personas for Everything, Groups

A group itself can be a persona; each unit is self-contained while also being connected to everything around it. This allows us to reduce a "group" of personas and project it as a single persona that is afforded the consensus of the group and has the potential to leverage the sum total of all the resources available to its members. Our notion of groups may be quite novel and the implications are potentially very interesting.

Ideally, OMS itself would guarantee that the group node could be trusted with total transparency into its process – enough so that the participants would all be equally represented and they would be willing to enter into contracts with high entropy-enabling flow-through mediating high-risk transactions.

Data Asset Market – Executable Contracts

Groups can be considered as a pattern suitable for enabling spontaneous and variably lasting markets by connecting institutions with transferrable data rights. That is, a Group TCC's policy manager essentially implements data rights exchange automation for distributing OAuth tokens to invited guests based on the credentials they were assigned by the acceptance of the invite (transfer of rights). This allows users in a chat channel to present themselves as authenticated and rootID-backed identities while leveraging attributes to specify their projection, from anonymous to completely verified digital identity. Within particular contexts, typified by shared social responsibilities or market participation rules, the Policy Manager is also expected to adhere to higher priority policies defined by the encapsulating Trust Network(s).

Looking at it from another perspective: we just want to be able to hyper-dynamically create, read, update, and delete (CRUD) networks of input/output sources and trusted computation. This takes us back to the problem of, "how do we get the best use out of the fact that the largest network is the one that moves the most data through it (and that means being able to connect everything to it and allow each of those things to self assert their identity), provide some verifiable measure of trust?"

This allows someone to walk into a restaurant, class room, client, hotel room, theme park, of the future and experience "bring your device to work" qualified security and have all the video cameras, keyboards, monitors, temperature sensors, microphones, every I/O device under rootID hardware. In the ideal world you get this much control over your data by being able to deploy your private infrastructure yourself or through a trusted third party who maintains it in a way that they provably cannot access, imped or otherwise destroy your data.

Conclusion

Open Mustard Seeds is an open platform as service intended to provide a powerful new self-deploying and self-administrating infrastructure layer for the Internet, which gives individuals control over their identities and their data, and which enables the formation and self-governance of Decentralized Autonomous Organizations, Authorities and Enterprises to enable the creation and exchange of "digital assets." At the same time, OMS provides a framework for the autonomous regulation and enforcement of diverse global data protection and financial policies.

Moreover, OMS enables the definition, deployment, operationalization and enforcement of Trust Frameworks at scale to enable Data Ecologies based upon transparency and trust. OMS meets not just the aspirational intentions of the Consumer Data Bill of Rights; it is fully operational, autonomous and scalable. It addresses many long-standing and confounding institutional issues such as "who guards the guards" and the "principal/agent problem." It also solves issues related to the chain of custody for identity verification and interoperability, and respect for context and data-minimization.

OMS differs significantly from other approaches in that it is self-deploying, self-healing, self-governing and self-enforcing and -correcting. It uses contracts not only to express and assert rights but to control how they are expressed. This is achieved through control over permitted data attributes and through the configuration, logging and correction of processes and VMs. Like the Bitcoin protocol, it uses algorithmic oversight and signing in preference to human intervention to enable efficiency, scale, performance, integrity, transparency and open innovation. It is based upon many open source bundles based upon the M.I.T. X11 open source license.

Notes

[1] Over the last ten years there have been many concerted efforts to deal with identity, authentication, and federation of access issues on the Internet and give users control over their personal data. Some the efforts related to this work include Microsoft's Kim Cameron's Laws of Identity, at http://www.identityblog.com); Project Higgins, a project started at the Berkman Center (http://www.eclipse.org/higgins); an industry consortium, Kantara (https://kantarainitiative.org); Project VRM, also started out of Harvard's Berkman Center (Project VRM, at http://blogs.law.harvard.edu/vrm/); OpenID Connect (http://openid.net/connect); and more recently, from the Human Dynamics Group at the M.I.T. Media Lab, Open PDS (http://openpds.media.mit.edu).

[2] The approach to a Trust Framework is similar in principle to that proposed by the Open Identity Exchange (OIDX, at http://openidentityexchange.org/what-is-a-trust-framework) and the Open Identity Trust Framework (OITF) model with an important difference. The OIDX approach is based upon a loose set of industry principles and is not really open but is captive to the interests of its board and members. The Trust Framework presented here is an actual platform and an instance of Distributed Autonomous Organization.

[3] National Strategy for Trusted Identities in Cyberspace (NSTIC) is part of NIST (National Institute of Standards and Technology). See the website http://www.nist.gov/nstic.

[4] Mihaela Ulieru and Rene Doursat, "Emergent Engineering: A Radical Paradigm Shift," *International Journal of Autonomous and Adaptive Communication Systems* (IJAACS), 4(1) (2011).

[5] Much of the initial work on getting personal data for predictive analytics was initiated at the M.I.T. Media Lab by Nadav Aharony (http://nadav.media.mit.edu/index.html%3Fn=Projects.Funf.html), which also triggered the development of

OpenPDS by Yves-Alexandre de Montjoye, at http://www.demontjoye.com/
projects.html.

[6] We are fortunate to leverage the open source version of OpenID Connect and
OAuth 2.0 developed by Justin Richer of MITRE Corp., which is now being supported by the M.I.T. Kerberos and Trust Consortia. We did make modifications
of the MITRE version to support Personas.

[7] IBM's IDMIxer (http://researcher.watson.ibm.com/researcher/view_group.
php?id=664) and Microsoft's Uprove technology (http://www.microsoft.com/
mscorp/twc/endtoendtrust/vision/uprove.aspx) provide zero knowledge
proofs for protecting personal identity while providing requisite authentication.

Chapter 15

The Necessity of Standards for
the Open Social Web

By Harry Halpin

FOR THE FIRST TIME IN HUMAN HISTORY, the majority of our social communication – from our beloved photographs to our most intimate of chatter – is being captured by digital platforms, most of them closed and proprietary "social" platforms like Facebook and Google. This is a relatively recent but profound shift in the historical playing field, a massive digital accumulation and colonization of social life seemingly without bounds.

This epochal shift is dramatic, but not especially surprising. The adoption of new languages and linguistic techniques – the process of *grammatization* – has long been at the center of profound political transformations.[1] In Europe, the great transition from feudalism to capitalism was intertwined with the transition in governance from monarchy to the nation-state – a transformation that itself was grounded in the spread of literacy amongst the former peasants.

For generations, Latin could be read only by the clergy, a fact that served to marginalize the vast majority of the population. Yet with "industrialization of language" made possible by the printing press, literacy escaped the confines of the church and spread across the wider social realm. This social reality enabled many more people to engage in the "Republic of Letters" that constituted the foundation of the Enlightenment. Let us not forget that something as simple as the mass production of a Bible, in no small part due to Gutenberg's invention, was enough to cause religious wars throughout Europe.

Yet mass literacy also paved the path for a new civilization: Whoever thought that the formerly illiterate masses would self-organize the French Revolution? Bernard Stiegler points out the striking parallels of the digital revolution for our times. We live at the very brink of a similar cataclysm, Stiegler argues, as our very language – and eventually political and economic institutions – is digitized before our very eyes.[2] The algorithms and code that increasingly shape and govern our social existence are mostly controlled by a small corporate oligopoly that, hand in hand with the secret state revealed by Snowden, has established a regime of exploitation and domination based on centralized control of digital communication.

Hope is not lost, however: A new vernacular of our digital age – open standards – offers enormous potential for assuring that freedom and innovation can flourish. Open standards are critical because they prevent anyone from gaining unfair advantages or control over commerce, politics and other realms of life. Anyone is able to create new code and to access data, much as people during the Enlightenment acquired the capacity to access knowledge in their native languages.

The social impact of a new, accessible language of code is not hard to imagine. The Internet and Web are living examples of the catalytic power of open standards: TCP/IP and HTML serve as the literal building blocks of the Internet and Web, respectively, allowing any computer to join the Internet and any person to create a Web page. When anyone is empowered to contribute – not just credentialed "professionals" authorized by centralized, hierarchical institutions – the result is an explosion of creativity that can even overthrow governments: Witness Tahrir Square. However as witnessed by postrevolutionary Egypt, the hard problem is perhaps not the overthrow of pre-existing institutions, which seems to come about all too easily, but how a genuinely new social – and today, digital – realm can arise without domination and exploitation.

Why Open Standards Matter

Large institutions are increasingly using Big Data to assert institutional control over our personal information and, in turn, what we can read, think, create and organize with others: The question is how to take that power back without losing its myriad advantages. To prevent the centralization of our data in the hands of a neofeudal digital regime and all the dangers that this entails, we urgently need to construct a new ecosystem of open standards to allow secure forms of digital identity that everyone from individuals to institutions can deploy without being "locked-in" to existing players. (See Chapter 13, "The ID3 Open Mustard Seed Platform," by Thomas Hardjono et al.)

These new open standards not only be limited to providing the functions of the current regime of centralized social networking providers (Facebook, Twitter, LinkedIn, etc.), but go further in empowering individuals to control their own digital identities and digital communications. Simply using these platforms "as is" will not enable a flowering of innovation because much of the core control over identity – and thus control over how people may interact – will remain in the hands of a few centralized players who control username, passwords, personal data, metadata and more. These players naturally wish to control how personal data will be used because so much of their current institutional sovereignty and revenues depend upon it.

Why shouldn't users be able to choose – and even create their own – self-sovereign digital identities? Why shouldn't identity creation and verification be based on open standards like the Internet? This is surely the best guarantor against abuses of the data. To achieve this vision, every element of a decentralized identity ecosystem would have to embrace standard protocols to communicate with other systems, much as all Internet and Web users must adhere to the TCP/IP and HTML protocols, respectively. Otherwise, users would be locked-in to their own system and unable to communicate with the rest of the Web. Ideally, even large social networking sites such as Twitter and Facebook would likely choose to use open protocols. If this were to be the case, those using open standards could even take advantage of the "network effects" of the tremendous numbers of users on these commercial platforms, while still having the privacy and power of controlling their own digital identity.

Based on the precedents of the Enlightenment, the Internet and the Web, there is a great likelihood that open standards for data would unleash a new digital enlightenment whose transformative effects we can only speculate about. It is clear that, faced with problems whose structures and complexity are difficult to grasp – global climate change, the financial crisis and the spread of failed states – we desperately need to harness the potential power of an interconnected world. Open standards for identity are the first step.

The Vital Role of Open Standards Bodies

Open standards such as TCP/IP and HTML serve as the literal building blocks of the Web and Internet, allowing any computer to join the Internet and any person to create a webpage. These standards were created by bodies such as the Internet Engineering Task Force (IETF) and World Wide Web Consortium (W3C), which rely on a consensus-making process in an open and evolving group of members. The processes followed by open standards bodies are quite different from those used by conventional standard-setting bodies at the national level such as the American National Standards Institute (ANSI) or international bodies such as the International Telecommunications Union (ITU). In contrast to the standards-setting bodies of the Internet, these pre-Internet standardization bodies normally use formal processes to adopt standards via majority votes by representatives of a closed group, such as nation-states.

This process – an *open multistakeholder process* – is never simple but seems to work remarkably well for technical standards. In light of the great success of the TCP/IP stack of protocols over the alterna tive ITU-backed network stack OSI (Open Systems Interconnection), an open multistakeholder process has proven itself to be superior to traditional processes in creating effective, widely accepted open standards. Perhaps most interesting is that multistakeholder standards bodies allow individual or institutional participation based on informality and merit, and not on the basis of political credentials or government roles. In the words of first Chair of the Internet Architecture Board David Clark: "We reject kings, presidents and voting. We believe in rough consensus and running code."[3]

The Internet has achieved its stunning technical interoperability and global reach by bringing to the table a complex social network of interlocking and sometimes even institutional adversaries, ranging from open source projects to companies such as Google and telecommunications providers. These institutions work together by agreeing to use a number of standardized protocols that are "loosely connected" (allowing for modest variations) and to respect the rather vaguely defined principles of Web and Internet architecture. [4] A mixture of hackers, government bureaucrats and representatives of corporations create and maintain these protocols via a small number of interlocking standards bodies such as the IETF and W3C. Through their technical protocols, these standards bodies play a vital role in defending the often-implicit guiding principles of the Internet and Web, such as net neutrality and the "end-to-end" principle, which are widely deemed responsible for the Internet's astounding growth.

When the Internet was first being built, the *Internet Engineering Task Force* functioned as an informal network of graduate students who posted "Requests for Comments" (RFCs) for early Internet protocols. Frustrated with the large number of incompatible protocols and identification schemes produced by the IETF, Tim Berners-Lee had the vision of a universal information space that he called the World Wide Web.[5] He built the Web as a quick prototype while working part-time at the European Organization for Nuclear Research, known as CERN. Berners-Lee sent the core draft specifications for his Web prototype (based on protocols known as URL, HTML, HTTP) to the IETF as "experimental" specifications despite the rejection of his original academic paper by the 1991 ACM (Association of Computing Machinery) Hypertext Conference.

The IETF declined to approve a "Universal" or "Uniform" resource identifier scheme (URIs), and large corporations started entering the IETF, potentially compromising the integrity of the standard-setting process. This prompted Berners-Lee to establish his own standards-setting body, the *World Wide Web Consortium* (W3C) to manage the growth of the Web. With offices in Europe, the United States, Japan, and even China, as well as a paid neutral technical staff of over seventy employees and a more formal process than the IETF, the W3C has managed to fend off monopolistic control of Web standards and foster the development of the Web, including the adoption of such technologies as HTML5.

The W3C and IETF now work closely together. In conjunction with ICANN, these standard-setting bodies serve as the core of the multistakeholder process of Internet governance described in the "OpenStand" principles (www.open-stand.org).

The standardization process is not only concerned with the technical development of the standards, but with fostering an hospitable environment for patents. In the United States, unfortunately, software patents have become so expansive in scope that even free and open source software is sometimes accused of infringing on a patented idea, triggering mandatory licensing fees to patent-holders. Since patented software has become a large industry, it is important for any open standard to be freely useable by developers without fear of licensing fees or patent trolls.

Open standards bodies such as the W3C are committed to standards policies that allow both commercial and open source software to use the standards and still interoperate. For example, W3C's licensing commitments to HTML5 allow both commercial closed-source browsers such as Internet Explorer and open source browsers such as Mozilla to render the same web-page in a similar fashion to users. This ensures that users are not stuck viewing the Web with a particular browser and that patent claims will not impede the future development of the Web.

The IETF deals with patents through what has been called the "Note Well" agreement. The general point is that "in all matters of copyright and document procedures, the intent is to benefit the Internet community and the public at large, while respecting the legitimate rights of others."[6] However, the IETF does not guarantee royalty-free licensing via legally binding agreements.

Given the high level of corporate competition in the Web, the W3C constituted itself as a membership consortium so that these legal agreements can be made (while inviting participation by open source developers, academics, government experts, and small companies via its "Invited Expert" process). These agreements essentially bind existing patents to the W3C, allowing the W3C to act as a "patent war chest" for all patents related to the Open Web and as a guarantor that patents will be licensed royalty-free to developers everywhere.[7]

The "social web" – websites dedicated to social networking – is currently a very fragmented landscape. It has no central standards body and a bewildering number of possible protocols and phrases. In order for a new layer of social and identity protocols to be incorporated into the rest of the Web via open standardization, it would be necessary, in an ideal scenario, to establish a single set of standards for each step in how digital identity and social networking are currently managed in existing closed, centralized data silos, and then adapt them to an open and decentralized world.

Open Standards and Digital Identity

Identity is the connection between descriptive data and a human or social institution. As such, identity essentially serves as the "digital name" of some entity. Particular ways of encoding that name are *identifiers*. Identity systems go far beyond simple natural language names such as "Tim Berners-Lee." Berners-Lee has a phone number which, with an internationalized calling code and a USA phone number, would consist of 10 digits. These digits are not connected to the Internet in an obvious way. However, with the advent of the Internet, a number of new identification schemes has come into being, such as email addresses like timbl@w3.org or even Facebook accounts like "Tim Berners-Lee" (https://www.facebook.com/tim.bernerslee).

Interestingly enough, while one's natural language "proper name" is in general registered and controlled by the government as a matter of law, identifiers ranging from phone numbers to e-mail addresses to Facebook accounts tend to be controlled by private institutions such as corporations. For evidence, simply look at what is after the "@" symbol in any email! This proliferation of identifiers that have no standard way of interoperating has led some technical observers to propose the establishment of an identity ecosystem in which the various identities and relevant data of persons and organizations could be integrated. This in turn would enable new services and more efficient transactions, while continuing to allow people the freedom to use pseudonyms or remain anonymous.

One strategy for achieving this vision is to chose a common identifier to bind together all of a user's identities, which in turn would determine who controls the identifier. The earliest technical paper to really broach the question of user-controlled identity and personal data is the 2003 article, "The Augmented Social Network: Building Identity and Trust into the Next-Generation Internet," by K. Jordan et al.[8] The authors proposed to "build identity and trust into the architecture of the Internet, in the public interest, in order to facilitate introductions between people who share affinities or complementary capabilities across social networks." The ultimate goal was to create "a form of online citizenship for the Information Age."

Although the paper was ambitious in scope and wide-ranging in a vision for revitalizing democracy, the concept was never taken to a standards body. Instead, an entrepreneur, Drummond Reed of a company called InterMinds, created a new kind of identifier called XRIs (Extensible Resource Identifiers). This protocol was designed to replace user-centric identifiers with a for-profit monopoly on identity controlled by Reed himself.[9] When Reed claimed on a public mailing list that there were patents on XRIs, Tim Berners-Lee called for them to be rejected, and the W3C intervened so that the proposed XRI standard was indeed rejected from the OASIS standards body (Organization for the Advancement of Structured Information Standards).[10] As an alternative, Berners-Lee supports the use of URIs ("Uniform Resource Identifiers," previously known as URLs or "Uniform Resource Locators") as identifiers not just for webpages, but for all sorts of things that could be connected to the Web. For example, Berners-Lee's URI would be http://www.w3.org/People/Berners-Lee/card#i. The idea would be to use URIs to leverage the infrastructure of the Web to enable even more versatile functions and services. Yet very few people use URIs to address themselves, and standards that embedded URIs failed to build a decentralized social web.

In response to the lack of uptake of URIs as identifiers, developers considered e-mail addresses rather than URIs for portable identifiers. The reason is simple: Email addresses are very personal and users remember them naturally, unlike URIs. Email addresses are associated with a concrete set of embodied actions, namely checking and reading email inboxes, and so are more easily remembered. While both URIs and email addresses depend on the domain name system, users do not actually control their own email addresses; the owner of the domain name does. So for the email address timbl@w3.org, the W3C controls the domain name on which it is hosted.

In the case of services such as Facebook, Twitter and Google, the identity of the user is completely controlled by the corporation and the user has no rights over their digital identity – a power that is even more controlling than that exercised by nation-states (over passports, for example). Corporations exercise these powers over identity even though they do not own domain names indefinitely, but lease them from domain registrars who ultimately lease them from ICANN – which has the IANA (Internet Assigned Names and Numbers Authority) function to distribute domain names on lease from the U.S. Department of Commerce.

On the other end of the spectrum, there have been successful attempts to create a fully decentralized identifier system based on distributed hash-tables. But none of the solutions like Namecoin or telehash has been standardized and both require users to use an indecipherable cryptographic hash instead of a human-memorable identifier for their identity. While Tim Berners-Lee may not think timbl@w3.org is a great identifier, he would surely balk at using *f4d-8b1b7f4e3ec7449822bd80ce61165* as his identifier!

The main purpose of an identity ecosystem is to enable the use of *personal* data: that is, any data pertaining to a particular human being or institution under autonomous control. Currently, social networking "silos" such as Facebook, Google+ and Twitter mostly trade in low-quality social data, such as names and lists of friends – as well as shopping preferences. However, there have been moves towards enforcing higher quality standards and verified personal data, such as the use of a "real name" policy in Google+. Google+ and Facebook have also sought to link phone numbers as well as geolocation to identities in their proprietary silos.

Notwithstanding these gambits, high-value data such as credit histories and medical records are to a large extent still controlled by traditional institutions such as banks and hospitals. The thesis put forward by the World Economic Forum in reports such as "Personal Data: A New Asset Class" is that high-quality personal data currently "locked" away in traditional institutions could serve as a valuable input into data-driven innovation.[11] This in turn could enable a whole new realm of efficient transactions and community-driven social innovation.

The vision is that users should control their own data via personal data stores, also called "personal data lockers." These personal data stores consist of attributes, such as full name, phone number, bank balance and medical attributes. Various systems can be used to double-check these attributes by various means, including machine-learning and background checks, all of which would be used to create verified attributes. By controlling their own data, users could then enter into contracts that would enable powerful services in exchange for their data. Users could also establish their own self-organized "trust frameworks" via algorithmically backed, legally binding agreements. (See Chapter 13, "The ID3 Open Mustard Seed Platform," by Thomas Hardjono et al.)

The act of claiming and then using an identity can often be broken down into two distinct elements: *authentication* and *authorization*. The first step, authentication, is when some proof of identity is offered, often thought of a credential-like password or even some secret cryptographic key material in a smartcard. Services called *identity providers* require authentication to access personal data, and may also associate (possibly verified) attributes with an identity.

Note that authentication does not necessarily reveal any identifying characteristics and so may keep the authenticating entity anonymous. One such effective technique is "zero-knowledge proofs," which allows a user to authenticate his or her identity without revealing a legal name or other attributes to the identity provider.[12] Of course, different kinds of identity providers or even the same identity provider may host different personas, and different levels of security may require different kinds of credentials to authenticate.

Right now the primary method of authentication is the username and password, but due a number of serious security breaches, this standard technique is likely to be improved. Current approaches tend to try to associate either some private cryptographic key material (such as that on smartcard or mobile phone) or even biometric data with a credential. Still, there are currently no open standards in this space for this approach. The W3C Web Cryptography API may eventually make high-value authentication an open standard by enabling lower-level cryptographic primitives.[13]

The second step of identification is *authorization*, which occurs after there has been a successful authentication of a user. With authorization, a user can authorize the transfer of attributes between services. The identity provider can provide personal data in the form of attributes to a *relying party*, the service that wants identity attributes. Consider the case of a user who wishes to log in to a new service and wants his or her profile – including name and picture – to show up in the new service. The user may authorize an existing identity provider such as Facebook to transfer identity attributes to the relying party. If not already logged into Facebook, this is typically done via having the user be redirected to Facebook and then authenticating to Facebook via a username-password using the proprietary Facebook Connect, and then asking the user to explicitly approve the relying party's access attributes stored on Facebook. After the user accepts the transfer of personal data, they are redirected back to the then-personalized site.

From a privacy standpoint, the identity provider (Facebook in this example) observes all personal data transactions with all relying parties and so is able to build a map of the user's web services. Worse, there is nothing technically preventing an identity provider from doing personal data transactions without the user's consent. Today, a number of open standards exist for authorization, the most prominent of which is OAuth, managed by the IETF.[14] A particular profile of personal data for OAuth is called OpenID Connect, which has been refined and extended by the Open Identity Foundation.

Given that users currently have no control over what data is being processed about them via authorized transactions, a set of standards are in development called User-Managed Access (UMA), which aim to put the entire flow of personal data under user control.[15] The combination of this suite of standards, still under development and needing considerably more work, has potential to produce open standards for authorization of personal data transactions.

One of the features of social networking is the movement of real-time data like status updates given as "activity streams" by sites such as Facebook and Twitter. While the traditional Web has focused on static content served via webpages, the social web is moving towards a "real-time Web" of heavily personalized content. While Twitter, Facebook and Google all have proprietary methods for real-time updating in their social networks, there have been a number of proposed standards to tackle the much harder problem of a decentralized real-time Web. The key of the real-time Web in the context of decentralized social networking and personal data stores is to dynamically update other nodes in the network based on social activities or the appearance of new data. The most popular format for open status updates is ActivityStreams[16] and a wide variety of architectures have been proposed for distributing and re-collating these streams. This standard-setting work, along with APIs that make it easy for developers to use, have commenced in the W3C Social Web effort.[17]

There has been far less research than needed on privacy and security in decentralized social networks. In fact, decentralized social networks are not *a priori* more secure than centralized silos, as the sending of messages between nodes in a decentralized social network reveals the social relationships of the users to a global passive adversary with much less trouble than a centralized social networking silo. Yet currently there does not exist a decentralized social network that doesn't reveal such valuable data via traffic analysis.

Hope is not lost: It is plausible that a decentralized identity system could be created that is even resistant to the pervasive surveillance of the NSA. However, this will require considerable new research and difficult implementation work, especially for anonymity measures like cover traffic, a way of shielding network traffic from global passive adversaries like the NSA.

One can easily imagine a possible future where, rather than having our digital identities controlled by either nation-states or major corporations, we control our own identities and determine how we interact digitally with the wider world. Access to our online lives has become such an essential foundation of our everyday lives that access and control of one's own data may soon be considered as completely natural by "digital natives" as control over one's own body is in any post-slavery society.[18] For the moment, this vision still remains ultimately utopian – something that exists mostly as a vision to inspire and guide a few programmers who are trying to correct our dangerous socio-economic trajectory towards centralized control over our social lives. Programmers dream in code.

Yet there are also reasons to believe that this utopia has a fighting chance of becoming reality. Open standards bodies like the IETF and W3C are taking up the task of defining new identity standards. The language of open standards that could serve as the new vernacular for our digital age is being created in the here-and-now by concerned engineers. What is conspicuously absent is a larger vision that can appeal to the vast swathes of humanity that are not already part of the technical standardization process, and so could galvanize a new social movement suited for this digital age. Strangely enough in this era of cybernetic governance, we are suffering from a failure of communication. Those who can comprehend the current dangers of having our identities outside of our own control and those who understand the latent potential for standards-based autonomous digital identity must surely at some point find the words to express themselves in a way that can be widely comprehended. After all, the revolutionary call for an open social Web is being driven by the self-same collective feeling that historically has driven innumerable revolutions before: the desire for freedom.

Harry Halpin is a Research Scientist at W3C/M.I.T., where he leads efforts in cryptography and social standards. He is also a visiting researcher at L'Institut de recherche et d'innovation (IRI) du Centre Pompidou, where he works with Bernard Stiegler on the philosophy of the Web. He holds a Ph.D. in Informatics from the University of Edinburgh and his thesis has been published as Social Semantics *(Springer, 2013).*

Notes

[1] Auroux, Sylvain, *La révolution technologique de la grammatisation* (Éditions Mardaga, Paris, 1994).

[2] Stiegler, Bernard, *Prendre soin* (Flammarion, Paris, 2008).

[3] http://www.ietf.org/tao.html.

[4] http://www.ietf.org/rfc/rfc1958.txt.

[5] Berners-Lee, Tim, *Weaving the Web* (Texere Publishing, London, 2000).

[6] The entire Note Well agreement – http://www.ietf.org/about/note-well.html – explains this in much more detail in RFC 53789 and RFC 4879. See https://www.rfc-editor.org/rfc/rfc5378.txt   and   https://www.rfc-editor.org/rfc/rfc4879.txt.

[7] The W3C Royalty-Free patent policy is publicly available at http://www.w3.org/Consortium/Patent-Policy-20040205. The entire standardization process is described in the W3C Process Document and is available at http://www.w3.org/2005/10/Process-20051014.

[8] Jordan K., Hauser J., and Foster, S., "The Augmented Social Network: Building Identity and Trust into the Next-Generation Internet," *First Monday*, 8(8), (August 4, 2003), available at http://firstmonday.org/ojs/index.php/fm/article/view/1068/988.

[9] https://www.oasis-open.org/committees/tc_home.php?wg_abbrev=xri.

[10] http://danbri.org/words/2008/01/29/266.

[11] World Economic Forum, *Personal Data: The Emergence of a New Asset Class* (2011).

[12] Fiege, U., Fiat, A., and Shamir, A., "Zero Knowledge Proofs of Identity," in *Proceedings of the ACM Symposium on Theory of Computing* (STOC '87) (ACM Press, New York City, 1987), pp. 210-217.

[13] http://www.w3.org/TR/WebCryptoAPI.

[14] http://tools.ietf.org/html/rfc6749.

[15] https://kantarainitiative.org/confluence/display/uma/Home.

[16] http://activitystrea.ms.

[17] http://www.w3.org/2013/socialweb/social-wg-charter.html.

[18] Berners-Lee, T., and Halpin, H., "Defend the Web," in *Digital Enlightenment Yearbook*, J. Bus, M. Crompton, M. Hildebrandt, and G. Metakides, Eds. (IOS Press, Berlin, 2012), pp. 3–7.

Conclusion
A Digital Manifesto: The Windhover Transition

A DOZEN WRITERS, HACKERS, RESEARCHERS, TECHNOLOGISTS, entrepreneurs and Internet activists met for a retreat in August 2013 at Windhover Farm in Jefferson, New Hampshire. The goal: to articulate a shared vision for a next generation social Internet that is trusted and responsive to human and ecological needs. Three days of discussion yielded a statement, "The Windhover Transition," which is intended as a discussion draft to provoke ongoing public dialogue. Another retreat was held in August 2014 at Windhover Farm; other retreats are contemplated in Europe and Africa.

The Windhover Transition

At this moment in history, as a planet and a people, we are engaged in a profound self-reinvention of unprecedented scale, opportunity and peril. We are hurtling toward a future for which we are wholly unprepared, which is being critically shaped by digital technologies, and the mobile Internet in particular.

The Windhover Transition is an open global community dedicated to imagining and inventing the principles, norms, technologies and institutions needed to make such a transition successful. Meeting this challenge requires new ways of seeing, thinking and acting. We see human endeavors as dynamic and holistic – as parts of larger, living systems, natural and humanly imagined, whose expressive, evolving elements constitute each other's identity and behavior. In contrast to some technological libertarian movements, we do not see the individual as the starting point or end point, or as set against or above the group. Rather, both the group and the individual are indivisible and mutually defining.

This perspective represents a profound shift in human awareness because it recognizes that our species is co-evolving with assemblages of digital and biological technologies that themselves are clashing with incumbent social and political systems. As this process accelerates, it is intensifying and redefining the very boundaries of human identities and our relationships to our own built artifacts.

One thing is certain: our species must identify new ways to act as conscientious, self-reflective stewards of a future that integrates our own well being and that of our fellow creatures, digital and biological. We urgently need to develop new knowledge for cultivating harmonious, vital relationships with natural and constructed ecosystems. This entails identifying and defending new definitions of sovereignty beyond the traditional nation-state and classic democratic institutions. In this quest, it will be particularly important to recognize the sovereignty of the individual-group to self-organize new forms of collective action in transnational ways.

The focus of the Windhover Transition is to develop generative social practices, habits of thought and technological design that are commensurate with the magnitude and velocity of challenges facing humankind. These new approaches are based on empirical and experimental evidence, not ideology or prejudice. The new approaches privilege open, accessible systems and rely upon scientific inquiry in the design and experimentation of new forms of governance and social design. Testing, questioning, revision and invention are central to this process of discovery and institutional transformation.

Such a worldview entails a comfort with incomplete, complex, competing changing and pluralistic perspectives. Attempts to know should be rigorous, even skeptical, but always open-minded and tolerant. This mindset is not about reduction and control, but about inclusion, sharing and empathy – while remaining wholly realistic about what works and committed to institutions that are accountable.

A Declaration for Innovation in Trusted Social Sovereignty

The following are some guidelines for the social technological design and innovation to further social sovereignty and sustainable self-governance.

1. *All peoples shall have a sovereignty* of equal and unobstructed access and control over the data, algorithms, sensors and other means by which their unique biological and behavioral identities are to be defined and recognized.

2. *All peoples shall have the sovereign right of global self-assembly for self-governance,* whereby any individual can form their own *Distributed Autonomous Organization* or *Enterprise* with others for the production and allocation of resources, goods and services.

3. *Distributed Autonomous Organizations (DAOs) shall:*

   - Continuously evolve to achieve requisite transparency needed to achieve both accountability and trust.

   - Continuously evolve to reduce transaction and coordination costs.

   - Use contracts and agreements that are self-executing and self-healing.

   - Keep open and secure logs of performance/activities of all members of DAOs to achieve transparency and to encourage learning and self-correction.

   - Minimize sanction costs and penalties to avoid litigation costs, adverse countermeasures and needless social disruptions.

4. *DAOs shall have the right to self-governance* using experimentation and the invention of new mechanisms for participation, governance, adjudication, dispute resolution, allocation of resources and proceeds, inclusion, exclusion and market exchange.

5. *DAOs* shall have the authority to issue digital currencies and form digital asset exchanges that reflect the values and interests of

their individual DAO, which shall be free to trade and exchange for other currencies of value.

6. *All peoples shall be able to rely upon an independent and open global commons* to provide the technological support for open digital identity, governance algorithms and metrics so that claims of authenticity about individuals, groups, things and processes can be independently tested and verified.

7. *All individuals and groups shall have sovereign control over their personal data* assets and their right and ability to move them easily from one Distributed Autonomous Organization to another. No DAO or other party should be allowed to coerce an individual or group to relinquish or share data or services that violate their personal dignity and agency.

Index